LOVE TALES OF ANCIENT CHINA

LOVE TALES OF ANCIENT CHINA

X. L. WOO

Algora Publishing
New York

Library of Congress Cataloging-in-Publication Data —

Woo, X. L.
Love Tales of Ancient China / X.L. Woo.
pages cm
ISBN 978-1-62894-204-0 (soft cover: alkaline paper) — ISBN 978-1-62894-
205-7 (hard cover: alkaline paper) — ISBN 978-1-62894-206-4 (ebook) 1.
China—History. 2. China—Literature. I. Title.
Library of Congress Control Number: 2016941152

Printed in the United States

Also by X. L. Woo

Two Republics in China, Algora 2014

Old Shanghai and the Clash of Revolution, Algora 2013

Empress Wu the Great, Tang Dynasty China, Algora 2008

Empress Dowager Cixi: China's Last Dynasty, Algora 2002

The Four Beauties of ancient China:

Upper Left: Diao Chan, Right: Yang Yuhuan

Lower Left: Xi Shi, Right: Wang Zhaojun

TABLE OF CONTENTS

CHAPTER 1. IMPERIAL CONCUBINE YANG

The four famous beauties

Chinese history speaks of four legendary beauties who caught the eye of the ruling emperor in their respective eras. However, like Helen of Troy, despite all their charms, they were likely to bring trouble as well as delight.

The earliest of the four beauties was Xi Shi (d. 448 BC). Legend says that when she went to wash her fine clothes in a nearby stream, the fish in there, stunned by her beauty, simply sank to the bottom of the stream.

Xi Shi lived in a village in the present Zhejiang province, in an area belonging to the State of Yue in the earliest Warring States Period (472 BC–221 BC). As a result of one of the wars, the State of Yue was defeated by the State of Wu and the king of the State of Yue wanted to take revenge. His famous courtier Fan Li had a plan and he went around to round up beautiful girls. One day he came across Si Shi, by the water's edge. Her beauty struck the courtier. He took her to the palace, and she was trained to sing and dance. Then she was sent to the palace of the State of Wu. The king of the State of Wu liked the girl very much, and was so enchanted that he made her his queen and watched her sing and dance every day.

While the king of the State of Wu was thus neglecting state affairs, the king of the State of Yue secretly gathered and trained his army till one day he decided he was strong enough to invade the State of Wu. He conquered it; and then he thought of the beauty Xi Shi and wanted to send for her for his own enjoyment. But she was nowhere to be found. History suggests that the loyal courtier Fan was afraid that the king of the State of Yue would fall into the very trap they had laid for their enemy, and so he took Xi Shi away to where the king could not find her. Fan later became a rich businessman, and as it happens he and Xi Shi died in the same year.

The second great beauty in Chinese history was Wang Zhao-jun (52 BC–19 BC), of the West Han Dynasty (206 BC–AD 8). She was sent to marry the Mongolian prince and had to travel to his capital. It was said that while she was on her way, escorted to her new home, the wild geese in the north looked down and were so overwhelmed by her beauty that they fell from the sky.

How did it happen that such a treasure of a girl was sent away? While in her teens, Wang was selected to be a palace maid. All the maids in the palace sought to catch the eye and win the preference of the Emperor and be made an imperial concubine. They would ask the palace painter Mao Yanshou to enhance their portraits that were sent to the Emperor so he could choose the prettiest ones as his imperial concubines. Most of the maids bribed the painter, but Wang refused to bribe him, so that he painted her portrait with some facial defects.

She was of course not to remain as a maid. When the Mongolians in the north made war against the Han Dynasty, as they tended to do, to maintain peace along the border the Han Dynasty often held out an olive branch by offering to marry a princess to the Mongolian prince. Actually, a palace maid would be chosen and sent to Mongolia in lieu of a princess. This time Wang was chosen for the purpose. Before her departure, as a rule, such a girl would be summoned to the presence of the Emperor. Seeing her now, the Emperor regretted marrying her away. However, he was stuck—for the peace of the nation, he had to keep his promise. He killed the painter for deceiving him. And the lovely young woman died in Mongolia at the age of 33.

The third beauty was Diao Chan, who lived during the East Han Dynasty (AD 25–220). She liked to worship the moon goddess in the courtyard during full moon every month. The story is told that whenever she worshiped the moon goddess, the moon lost its sheen as if overshadowed by her beauty. Her family name was Ren and her given name was Hongchang. She was very clever and at the age of fifteen, she was chosen to work in the palace as a maid in charge of the Emperor's clothes and headgear. Her job title was Diao Chan, and that is how she is known in history. Except for certain specialists, common people don't know her real name.

When the palace fell into chaos, she escaped and was adopted by the high official Wang Yong (137–192 AD). At this time an evil courtier, Dong Zhuo (AD 141–192), controlled the court, with the Emperor only a puppet. He had an adopted son, Luu Bu (d. 199). Luu was the bravest knight at the time, but he and Dong were both lewd men. Wang Yong always wanted to get rid of Dong Zhuo and restore the power to the Emperor. He harbored a scheme, which the Chinese called the Beauty Strategy. First he invited Luu to his home for dinner. During the evening, he had Diao Chan come out to dance before Luu. Since Luu was highly susceptible, he immediately fell in love with the graceful young woman. Luu expressed his wish to marry the girl and Wang gave his assent. Only, he said, he needed time to prepare a dowry for her, which was only reasonable. Luu left in great ecstasy.

The next day, Wang invited Dong Zhou to his home for dinner. Again, he asked the girl to come out and dance before the guest, who of course was taken with her at first sight. Dong ordered Wang to send the girl to his residence forthwith, and Wang did not dare to refuse. A few days afterwards, when Luu came to ask to fix a date for his wedding, Wang told him that his adoptive father Dong had taken his future wife. This enraged Luu. One day he met the girl in Dong's garden and she asked him to kill Dong and marry her—and so he did.

But let's focus on the fourth great beauty. She was born in Yongle in the present Shanxi province, and her given name was Yuhuan (meaning Jade Ring). She became famous as Imperial

Concubine Yang (AD 719–756). Hers was a big and successful family, and they had a huge residence divided into three sections. The front section held the servant quarters. The middle section was the main living part for family members. The last section was the place for worshiping the ancestors. They had a large garden in the back of the residence with an artificial lake and a zigzag bridge over it. There were grottoes and some pavilions dotted here and there among flowers and trees. This was typical Chinese architecture for a big family residence in the old times. There was a small pond, later called Imperial Concubine Pond, below Watch-the-River Pavilion. It was said that the young Yang used to wash her hair in the limpid pond.

Her father, Yang Xuantan, was an official in Shuzhou but he died when Yang Yuhuan was ten. Then she went to live with her uncle, Yang Xuangui, also an official, in HeNan province. Generally, girls from the prominent families were well educated. They were taught to read and write, to dance and play some musical instruments, and to paint. Yang Yuhuan was particularly talented in dancing. She had three sisters, and one brother, Yang Gua, who was an official in the central government, while her cousin Yang Guozhong was a good-for-nothing. When he was young, he was despised by all the neighbors for leading a low life. Then he joined the army in Sichuan province and later was promoted to be a petty officer. But he was still poor. At the end of his three-year term, Yang Guozhong didn't even have the money to pay for his board and food in any inn to return home. Anyway, he often visited the family of Yang Xuantan, though Xuantan was already dead, and he had an affair with the second sister of Imperial Concubine Yang. That was her most active sister, Yang Yuyao, who was also beautiful. She was afterwards married to a man named Pei and gave birth to a son and a daughter for him, but Pei died soon thereafter.

She came from a well-to-do family, was educated and talented, and pleasingly plump — perhaps a rarity in China, but in the Tang Dynasty (AD 618–907) men didn't like girls who looked unfed! Legend has it that once when she was strolling in the imperial garden and touched some flowers, the flowers bent down, abashed to be outshone by her brilliance. So it was said that she had the ability to make flowers feel shy.

Yang Yuhuan's first marriage and the imperial concubine's scheme

At that time, the Emperor on the throne was Xuanzong of the Tang Dynasty (AD 618–907). He was the grandson of Empress Wu the Great. Now the Emperor wanted to find a wife for his favorite son, Prince Shou, who had already reached the age to marry. Generally, the Tang emperors would look for girls for their sons from the Wei family, Yang family, or Wu family.

Yang XuanAo, the uncle of Yang Yuhuan, had once worked as a matchmaker to select girls for sons of the imperial family, and of course he learned that the Emperor was looking for a bride for his son. Since Yang Yuhuan, his niece, was the most beautiful girl in the Yang family, he decided to make her the wife of Prince Shou. Through his influence with the new matchmaker, he succeeded in putting the name of his niece in the list of candidates. Rising to the surface like rice sifted from chaff, Yang Yuhuan prevailed through several interviews and was at last chosen to be the wife of the imperial son. She now crossed the threshold to enter the imperial circle.

The wedding ceremony of Prince Shou and Princess-in-law Yang took place in Luoyang city. They lived there less than a year and then Prince Shou took his wife back to ChangAn city, the capital, to see his father, the Emperor, in the tenth moon of AD 736. But he could never imagine that as soon as he arrived in the capital, he was drawn into a political intrigue by his scheming mother, Imperial Concubine Wuhui. This Wuhui wanted her son, Prince Shou, to be named the crown prince and was always looking for a chance to get rid of Crown Prince Ying, the eldest son of the Emperor.

In the eleventh moon of 736, Crown Prince Ying, along with Prince E (the fifth son) and Prince Guang (the eighth son), gathered in their palace residence and complained about their mothers who were out of favor with the Emperor. Yang Hui, the son-in-law of the imperial concubine Wuhui, came to know it and reported this to Wuhui. She found a chance to report to Emperor Xuanzong, adding that the three princes had formed a "clique." The emperor was very nervous about anyone forming a clique behind his back, afraid that they would plot against him.

The emperor fell into a great fury and summoned the premier to consult him about deposing the crown prince and other two princes.

The premier Zhang Jiuling (678–740) was an upright man. He pointed out that there was no evidence against them, and suggested His Majesty should not rashly make the decision to depose them. The imperial concubine Wuhui heard of this and sent someone to bribe Zhang, who refused the ploy and reported it to the Emperor. That convinced the Emperor not to depose the three princes. That time, Wuhui's scheme failed.

Some time afterwards, Wuhui created rumors about Premier Zhang and caused Zhang to be demoted. The next premier was Li Linfu (683–752), who was a wicked, sly person. To please the imperial concubine Wuhui, he often sang praises of Prince Shou before the Emperor.

In the fourth moon of 737, Wuhui secretly told her son-in-law to spread a rumor that the crown prince and two other princes were planning a rebellion. When the Emperor was told the rumor, he sent for Premier Li for consultation. Li said that when it came to the Emperor's family affairs, the Emperor could make whatever decision he thought fit. Therefore, the three sons were executed and deprived of their titles of prince.

However, after a few days, it dawned on the Emperor that there was something wrong with the case. He had killed three of his own sons without any evidence. He regretted it. Just then, Premier Li came to see him and reminded him that the position of crown prince remained vacant, adding his suggestion that Prince Shou should be the right person for it. The emperor didn't say anything.

One day a courtier, Pei Zhen, came to see the Emperor and said that he heard that someone had suggested Prince Shou should be made the crown prince. He reminded the Emperor of the fact that people were complaining that the crown prince had been wrongly killed. So it was not the right time to make Prince Shou the crown prince. Besides, through seniority, the elder brothers ought to be considered first. The emperor knew that this was correct. When Premier Li put up his proposal again to make Prince Shou crown prince, the Emperor said, "I won't select him."

The emperor had a favorite eunuch named Gao Lishi. Although a eunuch was low in social status, as a favorite eunuch of the Emperor, who often listened to him, he had great power. One day the head eunuch said to the Emperor, "Your slave understands that Your Majesty can't decide which prince should be the crown prince. In your slave's humble opinion, it should go by seniority." The emperor said, "You are right." In the sixth moon of 738, the Emperor declared his decision to name his third son, Prince Zhong, as the crown prince. The hope and plan of imperial concubine Wuhui came to nothing, and she soon died.

Prince Shou and Yang Yuhuan retired to their own residence and lived a peaceful life for the next five years. During these five years, Yang Yuhuan didn't bear any sons or daughters for Prince Shou. Readers may think that Yang Yuhuan would thus lead a smooth life till the end.

The Emperor meets Yang Yuhuan in the palace

However, her fate was differently arranged. She was destined to give us a touching romantic love story. On the eleventh day of the tenth moon in 740, when she was twenty-two years old, she reached the turning point of her fate. That day, the Emperor came to Huaqing Palace on a short vacation, as was his custom. It was his twenty-second visit. But on the day, he summoned Yang Yuhuan to the Huaqing Palace to meet him. Why did he want to see the wife of Prince Shou there? Since his imperial concubine Wuhui died, the Emperor was not satisfied with his other women. To make him happy, his head eunuch went to the Yangtze River area to seek beautiful girls for him. At last, he found a beautiful girl by the name of Jiang Caiping, daughter of a doctor. She was so talented—she could read and write and was versed in poetry, a renowned poetess in the neighborhood. She could also paint, play the zither, and enjoyed chess. The head eunuch took her to the capital in the north. The emperor liked her very much and made her his Imperial Concubine Plum, because the girl loved plum blossoms. The emperor ordered plum trees to be planted round where she lived. But after several years, the Emperor grew tired of Imperial Concubine Plum and wanted someone new.

The head eunuch knew the Emperor best and hinted that Yang Yuhuan would be suitable as his next favorite. That year, Yang was only twenty-two while the Emperor was already fifty-six, an age difference of thirty-four years. When Yang arrived in the palace, the Emperor simply stated his wish to have Yang for his imperial concubine. Of course, Yang could not reject the Emperor, who could decide her life or death. After a few days' stay, Yang was allowed to return to her own residence, as she was still the wife of his son.

During her stay, the famous tune of "Rainbow-Colored and Feather-Adorned Dress" was played and Yang Yuhuan danced to the tune. When she left, the Emperor gave her a gold hairpin and a jewelry box inset on the surface with gold, silver, and jade specks.

Yang Yuhuan actually fell in love with the old emperor, and people are always curious to know why. The emperor could have been her father. The reasons were that, besides wielding so much power, the Emperor was a handsome man and also talented in many respects, while her present husband Prince Shou was not romantic and lacked talent. The emperor was skilled in calligraphy. Travelers can still see a tablet with his calligraphy on it, in XiAn city. The place is called Tablet Forest, and there is a whole collection of tablets there. He also liked to compose music and could play musical instruments, especially a kind of drum called the Jie Drum, beautifully. A Jie drum was made of wood, somewhat round like a barrel, but thinner in the middle. The two ends were covered with dried goat skin. It was placed levelly on a shelf and was played on both ends with two drumsticks. Yang Yuhuan could dance to the beating of the drum played by the Emperor. They could perform music together as a couple in spite of the great age difference. They had true love between them and so handed down to us the moving love tale.

Yang Yuhuan's second marriage

One would hardly think that the next step for Yang Yuhuan would involve becoming a Taoist.

In the Tang Dynasty, morality regarding marriage was loose. The emperor's grandmother Empress Wu the Great (the subject of an earlier book by this author) became a nun after her first husband died and before she married her second husband, who was actually her first husband's son. Therefore, the Emperor followed this example, with a little change, and so Yang Yuhuan became a female Taoist in the imperial temple. What is the difference between a nun and a Taoist? Besides the different clothes, a nun must shave off all her hair, while a Taoist put up her hair in a knot. When a nun wants to shift back to being a lay person, she must let her hair grow long, while a Taoist can easily shift back by just letting her hair down. So the Emperor chose to have Yang Yuhuan take the easy way.

When Yang Yuhuan was back home, she felt uncomfortable. But Prince Shou knew nothing about what had happened and he spent his days as usual. The emperor was more restless and wanted to have the beauty beside him right away. Anyway, that a father-in-law should have taken his daughter-in-law by force was really a scandal, though no one could say "no" to him. It was better to get her in a roundabout way. So Yang Yuhuan became a female Taoist in the imperial temple, belonging to the imperial family. And her Taoist name was Taizhen. So sometimes people called her Yang Taizhen. Before the Emperor took Taizhen to his palace, he found another wife for his son to comfort him.

In the winter of 741, Taizhen went with the Emperor to Huaqing Palace on Mt. Li, where there was a hot spring for bathing. So Huaqing Palace was also called Huaqing Pond, as it had a small artificial pond for bathing. This time, the Emperor and Taizhen had a longer visit, from the 19th day of the tenth moon to the 14th day of the eleventh moon. This time, when the Emperor went back, he took Yang Taizhen with him to his residence—Xingqing Hall, not to the temple. From then on, Yang Taizhen began to live with the Emperor, though she didn't get the title of imperial concubine yet. The emperor was still afraid of gossip among the people.

After three years of living together, the Emperor at length conferred the title of imperial concubine on Yang Taizhen. That was in 745, after the Emperor had appointed the daughter of the courtier Wei Zhaoxun to be his son Prince Shou's next wife. In the feudal society of China, an emperor could do anything he liked. He could take his son's wife to be his concubine. He could also make the daughter of any courtier the wife of the son of another courtier. The parents could not refuse. On the contrary, they had to think it was a great honor to them and had to thank the Emperor. If the son and the daughter could not get along, well, that was their fate. They could not complain against the Emperor.

The emperor gave his son a new wife as compensation, and then he had the right to declare his son's former wife to be his new imperial concubine. There was no empress anymore. Anyway, the Emperor didn't make Yang an empress, and in reality, Yang enjoyed the same status in the palace as an empress.

Before Imperial Concubine Yang entered the palace, Imperial Concubine Plum had been the favorite of the Emperor. But as time elapsed, her beauty gradually faded. When Imperial Concubine Yang arrived, beautiful and young, the Emperor's favor transferred readily to Imperial Concubine Yang. Besides, it was said that Imperial Concubine Yang resembled a little the deceased Imperial Concubine Wuhui. So Imperial Concubine Plum was ignored and led a lonely and quiet life.

One night, the Emperor went to sleep alone in West Cuihua Pavilion. He suddenly thought of Imperial Concubine Plum and sent a eunuch to fetch her there. They lay side by side in bed, resuming their former heart-to-heart talk. Then Imperial Concubine Yang heard what was going on and rushed to the pavilion. Fearing that the two women might quarrel or even fight, the Emperor bade Imperial Concubine Plum to hide somewhere in the room. Imperial Concubine Yang dashed into the room and asked the Emperor, "Where is the Plum Genie" The emperor said, "In her own pavilion." Yang said, "Why not send for her and we can make merry together?" The emperor made no answer and ignored her. Yang began to cry and left for her mother's home. Before long, the Emperor thought of her and sent a eunuch to fetch her to the palace.

Once the Emperor thought of Imperial Concubine Plum again and sent a eunuch to give her a pearl necklace. She returned the necklace with a poem, which read like this:

> It's long since I've penciled my eyebrows,
> My tears smear my worn and torn red gown.

I've never put on makeup in my pavilion ever since.
How would a pearl necklace comfort me when I'm alone?

And how did Imperial Concubine Plum meet her end? Many years later, when a warlord from a Turkic tribe, An Lushan, rebelled and marched into the capital, the Emperor and Imperial Concubine Yang escaped southwest. Imperial Concubine Plum committed suicide by throwing herself into a well, fearful of being raped and dishonored by the rebels.

The rise of the Yang family

After Yang Taizhen became an imperial concubine, her former husband, Prince Shou, became her stepson. When he came to visit the Emperor, his father, if Imperial Concubine Yang was present, he had to kowtow to her and call her stepmother. A weird relationship.

As a rule, once a girl became an imperial concubine, all her family members would be granted titles. First, her deceased father was given as a posthumous honor the title of the duke of Qi, and her uncle, Yang XuanGui, was made the head of the department in charge of feasts. Her brother was promoted, too. And her male cousin, Yang Guozhong, such a low cad before, got promotion after promotion because he could flatter and please the Emperor. At last, after the death of Li Linfu, the former premier, he was made the premier. Yang Guozhong was hardly suitable to the position; he took plenty of bribes for appointing people to be high officials. His two sons married princesses.

How did he get such a desirable position? Yang Guozhong was fond of playing a kind of game called E-Pu. Each player had five chessmen and whoever managed to move the chessmen to the end line won the game. Luckily for him, the Emperor also liked to play this kind of game. When he found that Yang Guozhong could play so well, he liked Yang so much that he made Yang his premier despite his having no ability to run the country at all.

In the meantime, the Emperor was so fond of Imperial Concubine Yang, who was like his inseparable shadow, that he neglected his court. He stopped receiving his courtiers and discussing national affairs with them at the traditional levée (or morning reception). He entrusted everything to Yang Guozhong, who became the most powerful man of the time. No courtiers dared to offend him, as it meant risking misfortune or even death. Yang Guozhong gradually and unawares made a lot of personal enemies. His greatest and decisive foe was the warlord An Lushan. In the Tang Dynasty, a warlord was indeed the lord who administered a certain area but still obeyed the central government. Only he had his own army. He obeyed the central government solely in name.

As for Yang Guozhong, he was first appointed a staff official in 745, and then promoted to be a city judge to sentence criminals. In 747, he was summoned to the capital to be a secretarial clerk in the central government. In 748, he had fifteen titles, and four years later, in 752, he became the premier. He reached the peak of his life, with some 40 titles. The more important ones were the equivalent to: the chief prosecutor; finance minister; head of the central bank; chief librarian of the national library; minister of personnel; and minister of labor.

In the Tang Dynasty, female relatives of the imperial concubine would also be given honorary titles, generally Her Ladyship so-and-so. First, her mother was conferred the title of the Ladyship of Liang; her eldest sister the Ladyship of Han; her third sister, the Ladyship of Guo; and her eighth sister, the Ladyship of Qin. As Imperial Concubine Yang often thought of her sisters, they were allowed to move and live in the capital. But Imperial Concubine Yang could not foresee that her third sister would give her trouble once she arrived in the capital.

Lady Guo (d. 756) had the maiden name Yang Yuyao. She was a lovely young woman, but immoral. She had had affairs with Yang Guozhong, her own cousin, before she was married into the Pei family and gave birth to a son, Pei Hui, and a daughter. When she became Lady Guo, her son married a princess and her daughter married a prince.

As the three sisters moved into the capital, the Emperor took them as concubines, too, and gave each a big residence and often summoned them to the palace. They feasted and made merry together. The three sisters, especially Lady Guo, all gained favor with the Emperor. Before long, the lascivious Lady Guo became so popular with the Emperor that she caused great quarrels with

Imperial Concubine Yang. Lady Guo could even directly go into the palace without waiting to be summoned by the Emperor. A famous poet Zhang Gu wrote a poem about her:

> Lady Guo enjoys the imperial favor,
> She often rides into the palace at dawn.
> She's afraid make-up will sully her beauty,
> Only pencils her eyebrows lightly to see the Emperor.

She became another favorite of the Emperor, and even the daughters of the Emperor were afraid to offend her or the Yang family. Once two princesses did offend the Yang family, and the Emperor was so angry he took back all the gifts that he had given to those two daughters, and their husbands were expelled from government offices.

Now comes the end of the Lady Guo. In the rebellion of the warlord An Lushan and his successor (events that will be narrated in later pages), Imperial Concubine Yang and her cousin Premier Yang Guozhong both died. The other two sisters were also killed in the chaos. Lady Guo, her son and the wife of Premier Yang escaped from the capital to Chencang town. But the mayor of the town hated the Yang family just like everyone else did, since the Yang family members were known for scandal and corruption. When he was told that three members of the Yang family had come to the town, he wanted to catch them and began to chase them. Lady Guo killed her son and the wife of her cousin. She wanted to kill herself too, but did not succeed. The mayor had her captured and put in prison, where she languished until she died; and she was buried outside of the town.

The concubine, the warlord, and Li Bai

An Lushan (703–757) was a man who came from one of the Turkic groups in the north. He fought for the Tang Dynasty with great merit, so that he became a lord ruling over three administrative districts. At first, he and Yang Guozhong had joint benefits, but later, when An became a lord, Yang was jealous of him and started to hate him. Thus, Yang laid the foundation of An's rebellion.

As a lord, from time to time An had to go to the capital to report to the Emperor what was happening in his districts. Sometimes, he saw Imperial Concubine Yang with the Emperor. Like any man, he was also struck with her beauty. As for Imperial Concubine Yang, she was aware of the great age difference between the Emperor and herself. Generally speaking, one would expect the Emperor would die long before her, and she knew that the successor, any one of the Emperor's sons, would have not respect for her. She would need someone to back her up for her own safety. She thought that An was a man she could rely on for that purpose. Therefore, she often sent for An to see her when the Emperor was attending to national business. Gradually, they came to love each other as An was a young and vigorous man.

A legend about their love affairs relates that once during their love-making, An accidentally made a scratch on the skin of one of her breasts. Imperial Concubine Yang was afraid that the Emperor would see it when they were together, and so she put a piece of brocade over the spot as a decoration. Some say that this was the origin of the embroidered bra nowadays. Believe it or not.

Now, as fit as he was, An had a potbelly, and once the Emperor asked him what was inside his big belly. An cleverly replied that inside was his loyalty to the Emperor, who was very happy to hear it.

Imperial Concubine Yang liked to take baths and often went alone to Huaqing Hot Springs to enjoy the water. On her way there, her bodyguards would hold up long pieces of cloth on both sides to form a lane so that no bystanders or passers-by could see her in the imperial coach.

Sometimes she took An along with her to the baths. Once, after An finished bathing, Yang ordered her palace maids to put big swaddling clothes on him as if he was a baby. To flatter Yang, An began to call her "Mom." When the Emperor heard of it, he gave An a baby bath as a gift. From then on, An openly called Yang mom, but he never called the Emperor dad. When asked why, he said that where he came from, people only knew their mothers, they never knew their fathers. The emperor laughed it off.

Imperial Concubine Yang and Li Bai

Li Bai (701–762) was one of the best known poets in Chinese history. He was a poetic genius and people named him a deity of poetry. He also knew some foreign languages. Historians think that he was born in the present Kyrgyzstan in Central Asia (at that time, it belonged to the Tang Dynasty) and at the age of five, his family moved to Sichuan province in the west of China. The emperors of the Tang Dynasty also had the family name Li. Some historians think that the imperial family and Li Bai's family came from the same ancestors.

Li Ke, Li Bai's father, was an officer in Ren town. In 705, Li Bai began his education and in 710, he began to study all the Chinese classics. In 715, he began training in swordsmanship. He liked traveling and loved to drink wine, often until drunken. So in the olden times, almost every wine house put a placard on the wall, bearing these words: "Drink is the good habit of Li Bai."

In the eighth moon of 742, he went to the capital. As the Emperor had long heard his fame, he summoned Li Bai into his presence. Then Li had the chance to meet Imperial Concubine Yang, and whenever the Emperor and Yang went to Huaqing Pond, they would take Li along and would ask him to write poems for the occasion. Li became the palace poet, if this could be his title. But he was not a courtier nor an official.

A legend about Li Bai is relates to the Bohai State in the northeast of China, which was a vassal state to the Tang Dynasty. Any vassal state always wants to be independent; so they sent a messenger carrying the Credentials in their own language, saying that if the Tang Dynasty had such a talented man that could read their language and write a response letter to them, they would always obey the Tang Dynasty; or they would be independent. While the Emperor was holding court, he showed the Credentials to all the courtiers, but none of them could read the language. When Li Bai was told about it, Li offered to write the response. So he came to Court and translated the Credentials to the Emperor.

When he was urged to write a letter of reply, he put up some demands. Because he was so much better educated, he had offended some courtiers, including Premier Yang Guozhong, by looking down on them. The head eunuch Gao Lishi didn't like him, either. Now Li took this opportunity to press the point home. When he sat down at a table, he asked the head eunuch to remove his shoes so that he could sit cross-legged more comfortably. Then he asked Premier Yang to prepare his ink (by grinding an ink bar in water on a stone slab) so that he could dip his brush in the inky water and write. These were quite insulting requests. Anyway, Li did write the letter in the language of the Bohai State. The messenger, a fit deflated, conveyed the letter back to his state.

How Li Bai left the capital

Although Li Bai had offended some important persons, the Emperor and Imperial Concubine Yang still liked him. One day in the late spring of 743, the Emperor and Imperial Concubine Yang were in the Eaglewood Pavilion and enjoying the peony in bloom. The emperor summoned palace musicians and wanted them to sing something new. But Li Guinian, the head musician and singer, had nothing new to provide. Therefore, the Emperor sent him to find Li Bai so that he could compose new poems to the music. Li Guinian went to the wine house Li Bai frequented and saw him there, but he was drunk. Li Bai was carried to the palace. Imperial Concubine Yang bade a maid to sprinkle some cold water on his face, and presently, Li Bai came to, like from a swoon. The emperor asked him to turn out some new poems. So Li Bai wrote three poems to sing the praise of Yang. They read respectively in the following:
The first one,
>Clouds recall her silk robes while flowers recall her visage,
>Spring winds brush the railing, and dew is dense.
>If not seen on top of the Jade Mountain*,
>Will meet at Jade Terrace* under the moon.

The second one,
>A red peony with dew spread it fragrance,
>The Goddess on Wu Hill waited, heart-broken, in vain.**

---
* places where goddesses dwell.
** meaning no need to meet goddess when he had his Yang.

If you ask who is like her in the Han Palace,
It's lovely Flying Swallow* wearing her new dress

The third one,

Flowers and the Beauty are both happy,
They have the Emperor looking at them and smiling.
Spring breezes solace the Emperor in his sorrow,
As he leans on the north railing of Eaglewood Pavilion.

Then someone who had a grudge against Li Bai complained to Imperial Concubine Yang that it was not a good to be compared to Flying Swallow in Han palace, because Flying Swallow was not a good woman. So Imperial Concubine Yang began to dislike Li Bai.

Li Bai felt that it would not be good for him to stay much longer in the palace. The next year, he left the capital forever, and he started to travel again. He met Du Fu (712–770) and they turned out to be best friends ever since. When An Lushan rebelled, wishing to help quench the rebellion Li Bai accepted an invitation from Prince Yong, in the twelfth moon of 756, to be his counselor. But before long, Prince Yong offended the Emperor and was executed. All his men were taken as prisoners. Li Bai was exiled to the present Guizhou province in the southwest of China. On the way, he received a pardon. He was then fifty-nine. When he reached the age of sixty-one, he was told that General Li Guangbi was commanding a large army to attack the rebels and he wanted to join them, but he had to turn back when he reached halfway, because he fell ill. Next year he died and was buried at Dangtu.

A story about his death says that he was watching the bright moon, as he had written a lot of poems about it, but he was so drunk that he tried to pick up the moon as it was reflected in the river; he fell in the water and was drowned. A romantic death.

Quarrels and making up

When Imperial Concubine Yang found out about the secret meeting between the Emperor and Imperial Concubine Plum, she was jealous. The emperor was so fond of Yang that did not

---

* Flying Swallow was the name of the Queen in the Han Dynasty.

want her to be unhappy, so on the Double Seventh Night (7th night of the 7th moon), he met Yang in Longevity Hall in the palace. There is a legend about Double Seventh Night, which is told in Chapter 7.

On that night, the Emperor and Yang made a vow of eternal love, not just in this life, but also in every next life, till eternity. Further, to please the girl he loved so deeply, the Emperor ordered fresh lychee, which he knew was her favorite fruit, to be fetched to the capital by military dispatch on horseback from the south of China, the only place where it grew at that time. Du Mu, a famous poet of the Tang Dynasty, penned a couplet to describe this event:

> As a horse gallops through dust, the imperial concubine smiles;
> And no one knows that it's the lychee that is coming.

The poet's sarcasm lies there: the military dispatch should only be used for conveying urgent military messages, not to satisfy the self-indulgent taste of a lover.

How Yang twice offended the Emperor

Once, Imperial Concubine Yang had a particular quarrel with the Emperor. Generally no one dared to bicker with him, of course. Only Yang knew that the Emperor loved her so much that he would not hold it against her. But this time, the Emperor got furious and drove her away from the palace. Yang had to go back to her mother's residence. Anyway, after a while, the Emperor sent the eunuch Zhang Taoguang there to see how she was spending her days. Seizing the opportunity, Yang cut a strand of her hair and asked the eunuch to take it to the Emperor. Seeing this, the Emperor was scared, because in old Chinese tradition, if a girl cut a strand of her hair and sent it to the boy, it meant that she would have nothing to do with the boy any more. Their relationship would thus end. The emperor was afraid of losing Yang, so he sent his favorite eunuch Gao Lishi to fetch her back to the palace.

Imperial Concubine Yang offended used it just as a ploy to go back to the Emperor. So when Gao Lishi came to take her back to the palace, she was delighted and immediately got into the coach. And the Emperor and Yang reconciled.

The second offense happened one morning in the seventh moon of 746. She made the Emperor enraged, and the Emperor drove her away again. But at lunch time, the Emperor began to think about her and he refused to eat anything. His favorite eunuch wanted to assuage the Emperor and mentioned that since the imperial concubine had left in a hurry, she had not packed all the things she needed. Could his slave gather all the things and take them to her? The emperor gave his consent. He loaded her clothes, cosmetics, her jewelry, and so on and so forth, on one hundred carts. The emperor also let the eunuch bring her the foods she liked best. In the afternoon, the Emperor thought of Yang more and got restless. The eunuch implored the Emperor by continuous kowtowing to let the imperial concubine come back to the palace. So in the evening, Imperial Concubine Yang was permitted to come back. Yang admitted her wrong doing and begged the pardon of the Emperor. So the Emperor and Yang made up again.

An Lushan's rebellion

A rebellion started in 755 and ended in 763, almost seven years later.

At the beginning of the Tang Dynasty (618–907), their military forces were mostly centered round the capital for the purpose of strong defense. The farther from the capital, the weaker was the defense force. At the north frontier, the Tang government totally entrusted their defense to the minority groups there. So the local ethnic groups had their own troops. Since the Tang Dynasty had enjoyed long-time peace till the present emperor, the army was not used to fighting and the whole force had become weak—while the forces of the minorities became strong. The strongest army belonged to An Lushan, a nobleman of the northern group. He had an ambition to invade the Tang Dynasty and rule over it, and he was just waiting for the right chance.

Emperor Xuanzong, since he had taken up with Imperial Concubine Yang, had neglected national affairs and let the premier Yang Guozhong, the cousin of the imperial concubine, decide on everything. Yang Guozhong, had an ability to flatter, to please anyone he wanted to. As he had become the imperial brother-in-law, he did everything to please the Emperor and so he won the Emperor's deepest trust. Under his administration, the whole officialdom became corrupt. Common people led a bitter life and hated the Yang family. They wished that someday, someone would come to kill them all.

As An Lushan got stronger, Yang Guozhong felt a threat and was afraid that someday An would indeed come to endanger his power and safety. Therefore, he always bad-mouthed An to the Emperor. Thus, An felt that Yang was a threat, too. So An Lushan revolted using the excuse that he had to expel Yang Guozhong from the government lest he should bring more harm to the nation and the people. At that time, the Tang government had only 80,000 soldiers to defend the capital while An had 150,000 soldiers, as other ethnic groups also rallied to him.

An's battles with the Tang Government

On the ninth day of the eleventh moon, in 755, in Fanyang city, An Lushan declared his mutiny against the Tang government. Most of the towns and cities in the north were soon taken. When the Emperor heard reports about the insurrection a few days later, he ordered General Feng Changqing to defend Luoyang city, which was a strategic spot. If An wanted to come to the capital, he would have to occupy Luoyang city first. Then the Emperor appointed his sixth son, Prince Rong, to be the grand marshal and General Gao Xianzhi as the vice marshal.

Accordingly, An marched to attack Luoyang and, on the twelfth day of the twelfth moon, he entered the city. Generals Feng and Gao had to escape to a place that was even more important strategically, which was called Tong Pass. Later, the Emperor executed both for their failure in the defense of Luoyang city, and he appointed another general, Ge Shuhan, as the vice marshal in charge of the defense of Tong Pass, which was easy to defend and hard to attack.

On the first day of the first moon next year, An Lushan declared himself Emperor of the Dahan Dynasty. As Tong Pass was difficult to overtake, General Ge adopted the tactic of avoiding direct combat and simply stayed in the city. In the first moon of 756, An Lushan sent his son An Qingxu to assault the city, but he was defeated by General Ge. An's army was blocked and could not make any progress forward for several months. Then An Lushan thought of a stratagem and ordered General Cui Qianyou to conceal the strongest troops in the rough terrain, and displayed his older, weaker, or even sick soldiers where Tang's spies would see them. When the Emperor heard the false information that his opponent lacked robust fighting men, he issued an order to General Ge to take the initiative to assail the rebel army. Although Ge knew that it was a wrong decision, he had to obey, with sighs and tears for the predictable failure.

On the fourth day of the sixth moon, General Ge was forced to lead his army out from the city and attack An's army. An's General Cui laid an ambush on the south ridge of the mountains, where there was a narrow valley the Tang army had to go through. The Tang troops fell into the trap, of course. When arrows and stones came flying down from the mountains, the Tang soldiers had to scatter for shelter and many were killed. When Ge was defending his city, he had gathered 200,000 men. After this battle, he had only 8,000 left, with whom he retreated back the city. On the ninth day, General Cui occupied the city and General Ge escaped to a small town nearby. Finally, he was captured by An's army. Then An's army marched toward ChangAn city, the capital of the Tang Dynasty.

At the same time, a detachment of the rebel army was sent to attack Jiuyang town to the east of the capital. Zhang Xun, the general set to defend the town, had only 8,000 soldiers against 130,000 rebel troops. Many times, he fended off the assault of the enemies. He and his soldiers held the town firmly for three hundred days, which gave time for the government to gather troops. But he ran short of provisions and other necessities, until the day came when he had to kill his own wife as food to feed his soldiers. In China, during major famines, people would eat dead bodies. If they could not find any, they would exchange each other's babies. One family ate another family's baby. We are told that such things did happen in the history of China. However, as the enemies outnumbered Zhang's troops, Zhang at last fought to the death and the town was overtaken. Thirteen days afterwards, the government army finally came and subdued the enemies. The revolt thus ended.

Legends about the end of Imperial Concubine Yang

When the Emperor was told of the approach of the rebel army, he escaped south together with his family members and also Imperial Concubine Yang and Yang family members, guarded all the way by his imperial bodyguards. One day when they reached the place called Makuipo, the soldiers killed Yang Guozhong, the premier and cousin of Imperial Concubine Yang, as they had long held a grudge against the Yang family. Next, they killed all the Yang family members, but they were not satisfied and demanded that the Emperor let the imperial concubine die as well. They were afraid that if she was still alive when peace was restored, she would surely revenge the death of her family members. Their leader General Chen put the demand to the Emperor, who, for his own safety, had to agree. So Imperial Concubine Yang hanged herself on a tree and was buried on the spot. But after the rebel army was conquered and peace was restored, the Emperor went back to the capital. Then he sent his favorite eunuch there to carry the body of the imperial concubine Yang back to the capital and re-bury her among the imperial graves. When the temporary tomb was dug open, there was no corpse seen. It was empty.

Therefore, the Emperor thought that Yang was not dead but had gone to the islands to live with goddesses there. Chinese people in the ancient times believed that there were islands in the East Sea on which dwelt goddesses. Then the Emperor asked a Taoist from Linqiong to search for the soul of the Imperial Concubine Yang from heaven to the nether world, including those islands on the sea. Then the legend as described by a famous poet is provided at the end of this tale.

Another legend about her fate says that when the Emperor ordered the death of Imperial Concubine Yang, because of her beauty one of the bodyguards took Yang away and they hid somewhere and led a common life as an ordinary couple. That's why the temporary tomb was empty.

And still another tale, coming from Japan, suggests that the bodyguards' leader General Chen could not harden his heart to kill such a beautiful woman and had one of her maids die instead. Then he secretly had someone escort Yang to Japan, where she was warmly welcomed as an imperial concubine from the Tang Dynasty. She lived there for thirty years more and died at the age of sixth-eight. The famous Japanese movie star Momoe Yamaguchi declared that she was the descendant of the imperial concubine Yang.

Many renowned poets of the Tang Dynasty and subsequent dynasties wrote poems about the beauty of Imperial Concubine Yang. The most famous long poem was written by Bai Juyi of the Tang Dynasty (772–846), titled "Song of Everlasting Regret," and it reads as follows:

> The Emperor of Han preferred women of great beauty,
> He sought them out for years but in vain.
> A girl in the Yang family was just growing up,
> Not known to anyone, being raised in deep seclusion.
> Born too beautiful to be given away easily,
> She was eventually chosen to sit beside the Emperor.
> One glance from her beamed one hundred kinds of charm,
> And the beauty of all the ladies in the six palaces* was overshadowed.
> In still cold spring she was granted a bath in the pool of Huaqing**,
> Her smooth skin bathed in the warm spring water.
> So delicate, she was helped up by her maids,
> That's the first time she enjoyed the love of the Emperor.
> Cloud-like hair, flower-like face, golden dangling ornaments,
> *Spring**** nights all spent under the warm lotus canopy.
> The night was too short and the sun rose high,
> The emperor neglected his morning levee ever since.
> Pleasing and waiting on the Emperor at feasts, she had no moment to spare,
> Outings to the spring every day, sleeping with the Emperor

---

* Six palaces denoted the living quarters of the Emperor's women collectively.
** Huaqing is the name of a place where there is a bathing pool for the imperial family.
*** The Chinese character spring can imply sex.

every night.

The emperor had three thousand fair ladies in the harem

But his love of all the three thousand centered on one.

In the golden boudoir she made herself up for the evening,

After a feast in the jade pavilion she's intoxicated by *spring**
action.

Her brothers and sisters all were all given fiefs,

Her family was admirably endowed with Imperial glory.

So much so, that all the parents under heaven

Wished to have girls instead of boys.

The palace on Li Mountain towered high into the clouds,

The fairy music carried by the wind, heard everywhere.

Charming songs, graceful dances with string and bamboo
instruments,

The emperor could not enjoy enough all day long.

The war drums came from Yuyang**, shaking the ground,

Breaking the "Melody of Rainbow Dress and Feather
Garments."***

Smoke plumes and dust clouds rose from nine gates**** of the
capital,

Thousands of coaches and horses marching southwest.

With emerald coach canopies swaying, they moved, then
stopped.

Only a hundred miles west outside the capital.

As the troops refused to advance, the Emperor could do
nothing,

And the sobbing beauty died in front of his horse.

Pearl-inlaid headdress fell on the ground, but none cared to
pick it up,

Hair ornaments of emerald and gold, shaped like graceful
birds, and jade hairpins.

The emperor couldn't save her, only covering his face.

---

* Ibid
** Yuyang is the name of a place where a rebellion happened.
*** The Melody of Rainbow Dress and Feather Garments meant the
dance with music performed by Concubine Yang. The emperor liked it
very much. When the rebel army came, he could not watch the dance
any more.
**** Nine gates meant that the capital city had many gates and also could
mean that there were gates after gates to the palace.

Looking back, he saw tears and blood flowing.

Yellow dust floated up in the air, the wind soughing,

They scaled to Sword Pavilion* on a zigzag wooden board
way up into clouds.

At the foot of E-Mei Mountains** travelers are seldom seen,

While the banners lose brightness and the sun looks pale.

The river of Shu*** is green and the mountains of Shu9 are blue,

The mood of the Emperor morning and evening can be
imagined.

In the temporary palace as the Emperor watches the moon,
its light seems grievous.

In the night rain, the sound of bells is heart-rending.

Like heaven and earth whirling, the dragon coach**** returning,

But at that moment, he hesitated to leave there.

In the earth at the foot of Mawei Mound*****

There's no body of the buried beauty seen.

Emperor and courtiers look at each other, their clothes wet
with tears;

Their horses canter eastward to the gate of the capital.

When he arrived, the pond and gardens still looked the same,

Also the peonies in Taiye Pond and willows in Weiyang
Palace.

Her face like the peonies and her eyebrows like willow leaves,

Confronting these, how can the tears not be trickling?

Also on the day when the blooms of peach and plum blow
in spring,

And at the time when the leaves of Chinese parasol fall in
autumnal rains.

Clumps of autumnal grass lie in heaps in western and southern palaces,

And the ruddy fallen leaves all over the steps no one swept.

The performers of the imperial troupe have new white hair

---

* Sword Pavilion is the name of a place in the present Sichuan Province.
** E-Mei Mountains are in the Sichuan Province, on which there are
many temples.
*** Shu is the nickname of Sichuan Province.
**** The Dragon coach was used only by the Emperor. The dragon in
China was the imperial emblem.
***** Mawei Mound was the name of the place where the concubine Yang
was forced to die.

growing.

The eunuchs and maids in her former chamber become old.

As fireflies dart in the evening hall, the thought of her steals in,

When the wick in the single lamp burns out, sleeplessness goes on.

The night grows long and the morning bell and drum sounds late,

Day is breaking and though the Milky Way is still seen across the sky.

The dews dense on the cold tails of mandarin ducks,

The emerald green quilts also cold when one sleeps alone.

During the lasting separation of life and death, the years drag on,

Her ghost has never come into the dream of the survivor.

The Taoist from Linqiong* was the visitor to Hongdu**,

Who can summon the ghost with his spirit of earnestness.

Touched by the whole-hearted thinking of the Emperor

The Taoist sets his heart on searching for her ghost far and wide.

He rides on the air into the other space as swift as lightning,

Exploring everywhere in the Heavens and in the other world.

He seeks in paradise and he seeks in Hades,

And her ghost is not there in either place.

All at once he hears of the fairy mountains on the sea;

The mountains are situated in the vast void.

The magnificent pavilions rise among five-colored clouds,

In which there are a lot of elegant goddesses.

One of them is called Taizhen***,

With snow-white skin and flower-beautiful face like hers.

He knocks at the jade door of the west chamber in the golden pavilion,

---

* Linqiong was the name of a place and Hongdu denoted the capital.
** Ibid.
*** Taizhen was the another name of Concubine Yang.

Asking Xiaoyu*, the maid, to tell Shuangcheng**, another
    maid,
Hearing the arrival of the messenger of the Han emperor,
Her ghost startled from the dream in the splendid canopy.
Lifting her dress, pushing away her pillow, she slowly steps
    forth,
The silver screen with pearly foil opens gradually.
With her piled-up hair tilting aside, just awake from sleep,
She walks into the hall in disheveled wreath crown.
Her fairy dress flutters up in the wind,
Like in the dance of rainbow-colored feather-adorned
    garment.
Her pretty face reflects solitude with tears streaming
Like a pear blossom in the spring rains.
She thanks the Emperor with a gaze full of feelings,
His voice and visage so far away after parting.
Thus ended the love expressed in Zhaoyang Hall;
But here in Penglai Palace the time is eternal.
When looking down back to the human world,
Can't see ChangAn, the capital, but mists and dust.
To show her deep feelings she can only produce the old stuff,
And wants to send the gold hairpin and decorated box,
She keeps half of the pin and box for herself.
That is: half of the pin gold, half of the box decoration.
If only our hearts are so sincere as gold and box so sturdy,
We'll meet either in heavens or in the world.
When parting, she sends words by the Taoist,
There's a vow in the words they both know.
That's on the seventh day of seventh moon in Longevity Hall,
They vowed to each other at midnight when none were near:
They wished to be birds flying side by side in the sky,
They wished to be two bough-interlaced trees on earth.
Heaven and earth, though everlasting, may have an end,
But the parting regret of theirs lasts without an end.

---

* Xiaoyu was the daughter of King Fucha of the Wu Kingdom in
the Eastern Zhou Dynasty. Shuangcheng was the daughter of Queen
Goddess in Chinese mythology. Both were used here to denote the
maids of Concubine Yang in the fairyland.
** Ibid.

CHAPTER 2. THE TALE OF THE WHITE SNAKE

This is a sorrowful love tale that is well-known in China. It has been turned into a movie and has been staged as a drama. But the movie "The Sorcerer and the White Snake" has been modernized and is not true to the original tale, giving a wrong idea of Chinese literature. Here I give readers the true version of the story as I read it in my early boyhood.

Once upon a time, there was a young white snake who was sick and starving. She lay on the road side, dying. Then a boy went by, and seeing the lovely white living creature, he picked it up and brought it home. He fed it and nursed it till the snake was recovered. He then took it to where he had found it, and let it go.

A thousand years elapsed. The white snake became a snake genie with great magic power. One day, there came a green snake who had lived five hundred years. They began to fight over who would dominate the mountain. Since the magic power of the white snake was greater than that of the green snake, the green snake was defeated and swore her obedience to the white snake. As they could turn into human forms, they had a strong curiosity to know what it would be like to live in the human world. The white snake decided to play the role of a noble young lady while the green snake was her maid.

How the Snakes met Xu Xian

The boy who had saved the white snake had gone through many incarnations by now, and in this life he was a boy who had learned Chinese medicine. He was working in a drug store in Hangzhou city, famous for the West Lake. The typical image of Xu Xian is that he always carried an umbrella with him whenever he went out. Once he had been caught in a sudden rain and was soaked through; when he got home, he was sick for several days. He wasn't paid for the work days he missed. From then on, he always carried an umbrella outdoors.

At that time, employees were given a day off twice in a month. On his day off, Xu went to the West Lake to enjoy the picturesque scenes there. There were many boats on the lake and visitors could ask the boat owner to take them round for sightseeing. Xu lived on a small wage and could not afford the boat tour. He just used his legs for transportation along the lakeside for relaxation and enjoyment. It was a sunny day. But weather was changeable. All at once, without warning, a shower came out of the blue. Luckily for Xu, he had his umbrella with him.

Then he noticed under a nearby tree that two girls were using the tree as shelter from the rain. But they were still getting a little wet. Xu was a man with a heart of gold and often helped people in need — especially girls. So he went toward them and offered his help. The girl in white said, "Can you hire a boat for us so that we can ride the boat home?" He said, "Sure. Please wait here. I'll get one soon."

He walked to the wharf and helloed to a boat owner for a ride home. Then he went back to the girls and shared his umbrella with them. When the girls got on the boat, the girl in white asked Xu to come on board the boat too, so that they could thank him and have a little friendly talk. Xu complied. After a good while, the boat reached a place where a big house stood on the shore. The trio climbed out onto the bank and the girl in white invited Xu into the house for some refreshment. Xu followed them in.

Clever readers can surely guess that the two girls were the white snake and the green snake in human forms. As the white snake had magic power, she could know certain things. She knew that Xu had been the boy who had saved her life a thousand years ago. She wanted to repay the favor by giving Xu a better life. She planned to be his wife and bear a son for him. What would the son look like, a human head on a snake body, or a snake head on a human body? Don't guess this time, my dear readers, though you are clever at the first guess. The result will be revealed later, toward the end of the story.

The white snake gave herself a human name: Bai Suzhen, and green snake was called Little Qing (Qing means green). Bai produced a big house here by magic as she had planned. When the threesome entered the house, Bai asked Xu to sit in the living room at the round table while Little Qing went to the kitchen to prepare some food, also by magic.

As one may imagine, Xu had never had any contact with a surpassingly lovely girl, in fact, with any girl. And also one may imagine that the snake genie would herself into a beautiful, not an ugly, girl. So far so good. A little while later, Little Qing brought out delicious food along with some wine. Xu enjoyed the dainty food and pleasant chat, forgetful of the time, already late in the evening. After dinner, Little Qing came in to play the role of matchmaker as planned. Xu of course accepted the marriage, without knowing that his wife was a snake genie.

With great ecstasy, Xu passed the first night in his married life. He woke up late next morning. When he got up and had breakfast, he wanted to go to work. But his wife stopped him, saying that he didn't need to work anymore. After several years of hard work, Xu was glad to have a full rest. He now had free time to do what he wanted.

Caught in possession of stolen money

After a long while, he started to grow weary of his life without a goal, having nothing else to do but enjoy the days in the company of his wife. Knowing this, the snake genie offered to open a drug store for him, which meant that he would be the owner of the store. Xu happily accepted the offer. He went round the city to choose a suitable location. There was a bankrupt drug store the owner wanted to sell. It was at a good location and so Xu told his wife about it. The snake genie produced fifty taels of silver in a lump of a special shape, rather like a hat, called a yuanbao.

The yuanbao was used as currency in old China. A yuanbao could be either silver or gold. It could be divided into different weight: ten taels a piece, twenty taels, and fifty taels. Where did the genie get the yuanbao? She could not make it, nor could she earn it by working. She used her magic power to get it from the treasury house of the local government. Her husband did not know that; if he had known, he would not have used it, as it was looked upon as stolen money. But the snake genie was not familiar with the idea of the human world, "stealing."

When Xu used the yuanbao to pay for the drug store, he was found to be using a stolen yuanbao, with a seal carved on the bottom that identified it as belonging to the government treasury house. When this was reported to the local government, Xu was arrested and put in prison. He hadn't thought to check the yuanbao on the bottom. If never occurred to him that his wife could have had a stolen yuanbao. When Bai, the snake genie, learned the news, she did not know how to handle such things in the human world. She could not but wait and see.

A few months later, Xu was sentenced to be exiled to Suzhou city, another tourist attraction. Xu had an uncle living there, also owning a drug store. Uncle Xu knew that his nephew had a deep knowledge of medicine and had always wanted him to come to Suzhou to help him to run the store. Now as the nephew was transferred to the prison in Suzhou, he went to the local government to bail his nephew out. He paid a hundred taels for it.

Xu was released and went to live in his uncle's house. After a few days' rest, he went to work in the drug store. Sometimes he thought of his wife, left behind in Hangzhou. He did not know how to tell his uncle about his marriage. He was already of age when he got married and could do whatever he wanted, since his parents had died some time ago. He planned to get his wife to Suzhou when he had a chance, and then told his uncle of it.

By her magic power, she immediately knew that her husband had been released and now lived in his uncle's house. So she magically moved to Suzhou in a jiffy. She rented a house and went to see Xu in the drug store. She did not want to see the uncle first. She wanted to see her husband first. Xu was glad to see his wife again and took Bai to meet his uncle. Uncle Xu was happy to see his nephew married and to such a beautiful wife. From that day on, Xu moved out of his uncle's house and lived with his wife.

After a while, Bai planned to open another drug store for her husband again. This time she knew that she should not get yuanbao from the treasury house of the government. She produced some money by magic out of nowhere.

This time when his wife gave him the yuanbao, he looked at the bottom to see if there was any government seal on it. No such sign this time. He was at rest, but he asked his wife where she had gotten the yuanbao that had sent him to prison. Bai answered that her parents had left her some legacy in a money store (equivalent to bank nowadays) after they died. She went there to take one, but did not know how it could be a stolen yuanbao.

Xu went round to look for a drug store for sale and found one at a suitable location not far from home. He bought the store, all fully equipped. He hired some assistants for help. Thus they lived happily together.

The White Snake Genie and the Taoist

Taoism is one of the three main thought systems or belief systems that underpinned Chinese culture. With elements harking back even to pre-history, Taoism was developed more formally in AD 100–200. During the East Han Dynasty, Zhang Jiao used the religion to gather his believers, his followers, to riot against the government. Though his rebellion failed, the religion was adopted by people at large.

In old Chinese legends, a true Taoist had magic and exercised his power to catch evil genies that inflicted harm on humans. Whether a snake genie, or a fox genie, or any other form of genie, they all had something like a vapor about the body, invisible to common people, but a Taoist who had magic could detect it and know that it was a genie. If a genie lived with a human, the human also developed this something about the body. Let's call it *genie vapor* for convenience's sake.

There were some Taoist temples inside Suzhou city and in the vicinity. On the first day and the fifteenth day of every moon, people would go to the temples to worship the god and seek blessings. They would burn incense and candles, and kowtow to the statue of the god.

On one such day, Xu Xian went to a Taoist temple for the same purpose. The head Taoist in the temple detected genie vapor about Xu. He invited Xu to come into his room for a cup of tea. When they both took seats at the table, the Taoist said, "Mister, have you met with something or someone strange recently?"

Xu was curious and said, "Master, what do you mean by that?"

"Frankly speaking, I detect genie vapor about you. That's why I ask. Are you married?"

"Yes."

"How about your wife?"

"I met her months ago at the West Lake."

"So, you don't know where she came from, or what kind of family she has, right?"

"No. Nothing at all."

"I had a feeling your wife is a genie."

"What should I do now? Divorce her, get away from her?"

"You can do that. But she will track you down easily. She may not harm you. But it's not good to have a genie wife."

"Pray, tell me what to do."

Then the Taoist produced an amulet and handed it to Xu, saying, "Put it on your person. It will protect you from any harm. But don't let your wife see it." Xu took it and hid it in his garment. When Xu went home, Bai felt right away that there was some magical effect coming from her husband. But the magical effect could not do anything bad to her, because her magic power was greater than that of the Taoist, as she had almost one thousand years' practice. Nevertheless, she had to stop her husband from doing such things ever again.

That night, when Xu took off his garment to prepare for sleep, Bai pretended to accidentally find the amulet in his garment. She asked him sternly that this was. Xu was not a man to lie, and told his wife all about it. Bai scolded him and said, "What nonsense. Throw it away and don't go to that temple anymore." Xu had to cast it away.

Next day, when Xu went to his drug store, Bai went to the

temple, accompanied by Little Qing, her maid. When the Taoist saw the genie, he shouted, "How dare you to come to see me, you wicked genie!" Bai asked, "You have any evidence to prove I've done wicked things?" The Taoist was silenced.

Bai said, "Why you want to instigate my husband against me?"

"My duties in the human world are to drive genies out of the human world so that they cannot do anything harmful."

"You have to distinguish bad genies from good genies. You cannot treat both the good and the bad the same."

The Taoist didn't listen to her and began to use his magic on the genie. The Taoist flung out a dagger, which flew at the genie, trying to kill her. The genie took out her handkerchief, which flew out like a blanket and caught the dagger in it. The Taoist lost his dagger.

Then he took out a bell and shook it. The sound would make any genie feel dizzy and turn back into its original shape. The genie cast a stone towards the bell and cracked the bell into pieces, because her magic power was greater than the Taoist's. He could do nothing to harm her. The Taoist was helpless now. After teaching the Taoist a lesson, Bai returned home before Xu was back from work.

Xu has a terrible fright

It was soon the fifth day of the fifth moon, called Double Fifth Festival, in Chinese tradition. There were a few activities for the festival. Firstly, it was the special day in memory of Qu Yuan (seventh day of the first moon in 340 to fifth day of fifth moon in 378), who was a courtier in the Chu State during the Warring Period of the Eastern Zhou Dynasty (475 BC–221 BC). In that period there were seven states. There were long-time wars between the Chu State and the Qin State. Finally the King of Chu ignored the advice of his counselor Courtier Qu Yuan and was defeated. Qu Yuan was so sad to have his state conquered by the Qin State that he committed suicide by throwing himself into a river. On that day every year, there is a Dragon Boat contest, which symbolizes searching for and retrieving the body of Qu Yuan out of water. Another activity was to eat zongzi, which is made of sticky rice wrapped in bamboo leaves and boiled in water. This can be prepared many ways, varying in taste, sweet ones and salty ones. In ancient times, people made the zongzi for the purpose of casting it in water so that the fishes would eat the zongzi instead of Qu's body. Another ceremonial activity was to drink realgar wine; this practice has certainly been discontinued. Realgar (arsenic sulfide) has a smell that was believed to drive away all sorts of pests from diseases to insects, evil spirits, and reptiles, including dragons.

Although the Taoist had failed the first time, he would try to fight the genie once more. He went to see Xu in his drug store. He told Xu that if he wanted to know the truth whether his wife was a genie or not, he could have his wife drink some realgar wine on Double Fifth Day. On that particular day, Chinese people believed that if a genie drank realgar wine, it would show its original form. Generally, people would drink realgar wine at noon on that day, believing in its effect to keep people from bodily harm.

Accordingly, at noon, Xu offered a cup of realgar wine to his wife. She did not know such things and drank it to please the husband. She was soon drunk and lay down on the bed. After a while Xu came into their bedroom to see what was the result of the realgar wine. When he looked at the bed, he saw a huge white snake coiling on the bed, seemingly asleep. He was so frightened he fell to floor, dead.

A long while later, Bai came to from her drunkenness. When she sat up in bed, she was stunned to see her husband lying on the floor. She felt his body and found him dead. She used her power to produce a big mirror in midair, which showed everything Xu had done, from the Taoist going to the store to talk with him to how he gave her the realgar wine.

Though she hated the Taoist for doing such things to her, it was not the right time to go to the Taoist for vengeance. First she had to think of a way to revive her husband. She knew that there was a wonderful herb on the Kunlun Mountain in the westernmost region of China, where lived the god of longevity. There was a river called Weak Water that went around the mountain, and anything put on this water would sink to the bottom so that no mortals could build a bridge to cross it to the opposite side.

The snake genie could cross it by magic. So she did. Once beyond the river, she went along the slope stealthily to the top, where the wonderful herb grew in the residence of the god. She went there to steal a leaf of the herb which could restore life to the dead body. It was guarded by a stork genie, who also had magic power. The stork genie was a disciple of the god. When the snake genie slipped up to where the herb was planted, the god already knew she was coming. The god summoned the stork genie to his room and talked with him about how to practice more magic, so that the snake genie could steal the leaf of the herb to save the life of a mortal.

The snake genie found the herb and plucked one leaf. She put it under her tongue to carry it back. Accidentally, the leaf slipped into her belly, and into her womb. How could she have let the precious leaf slip? The god knew that the snake genie was going to give birth to a son to the mortal. If she did not swallow the leaf of the wonderful herb, her son would have had a human head on a snake body. Now the leaf had the effect on her so that she would have a son of the full human form. The snake genie took another leaf and quickly escaped to her human home in Suzhou. Once home, she smashed the leaf and put it in warm water. She gradually dripped the water into Xu's mouth and moments later, Xu opened his eyes. He had forgotten everything he had seen before his death. They lived happily together.

White Snake and Monk Fahai

On Mt. Jin by the Yangtze River there was a temple in which lived the head monk Fahai, who had magic power greater than that of the white snake genie. When Fahai became aware of the white snake genie living in the human world and marrying a mortal, he was upset. He believed that a genie should live in the depths of the mountains, not in the human world, nor even marry a mortal. So he went to Suzhou city and found Xu. He talked with Xu about his genie wife. Xu suddenly remembered the day when he had seen a big white snake on his bed, and he believed what the monk said.

"What should I do?" asked Xu.

The monk wanted Xu to go with him to the temple so that he

could protect him. Therefore, Xu went with Fahai to the temple on Mt. Jin.

Late in the evening, when Bai did not see her husband back home, she used her magic and found out what had happened. She and her maid Little Qing went right off to the temple. She wanted Fahai to release her husband immediately, but the monk rejected her demand. So they started to fight.

A head monk always carried a Buddhist staff with a carved-up end in various shapes. The monk cast his staff up into the midair and it changed into a dragon, pouncing upon the snake genie, which turned back to her original shape—a huge white snake. She flew up into the midair and fought with the dragon.

The dragon was really a staff, a thing without life. The snake hit it with her long tail and knocked it to the ground, turning it back to a staff. The snake changed back into human form. The monk had a rosary of beads round his neck. He took it off his neck and threw it into the midair. It turned to fire and came down around the head of the snake. The genie produced a vase with water in it. By magic the water in the vase gushed up, quenching the fire.

Then the genie raised up the water in the river and was going to flood the temple. The monk hurled out his cassock, which fell on top of the water and stopped it from rising. As the snake genie could not win, she had to retreat to find some other way to save her husband. The monk shouted to her, "You will see your husband on the Broken Bridge in Hangzhou soon." The monk knew that the snake genie was already pregnant and would give birth to a boy, who would be a government official when growing up. That's what Heaven had decided. He could not do anything against the decision of Heaven. So he should not do any harm to her at present.

The snake genie and her maid went back to Suzhou city. She planned to move to Hangzhou city. She produced a big basket and turned all the things in house into miniature forms like small toys. She put all the tiny things into the basket and flew to Hangzhou, with the maid carrying it all the way there. She got a house and lived in it, awaiting the return of her husband. Every day the genie went to the Broken Bridge on the West Lake to wait for the appearance of her husband. The monk had promised to send Xu there by magic.

By the way, why was the bridge named the Broken Bridge? It was said that in winter when it snowed, the snow covered the surface of the bridge. But the snow on the top surface was always blown away. So looking from afar there was a gap in the snow and the bridge looked like it was broken.

One day, at long last, her husband walked towards the bridge. The genie was glad that the monk had kept his promise. They met on the bridge. But Xu seemed to hesitate to come forth, since he knew now that his wife was a snake genie. The monk had told him everything about their relationship from a thousand years ago, and reassured him, so that he believed that the genie would not hurt him—she had come to him only to requite him for saving her life a thousand years ago. Besides, she was going to bear him a son. Anyway, when he saw her now, he was still a little afraid of her. Soon her warmth and pleasure in seeing him drove his fear away to the clouds.

A surprise at Thunder-Peak Pagoda

Around the West Lake, there are some renowned sightseeing spots, such as Su Dike in Spring Dawn (a causeway between Inner Lake and Outer Lake built by Su Shi, a famous poet and prefect of Hangzhou city in Song Dynasty); Lingering Snow on Broken Bridge; Thunder-Peak Pagoda at Dusk; Orioles Singing in Swaying Willows; Three Tans Reflecting the Moon (Visitors can see three "tans" on the water near an islet. When the moon is over the spot, the moon cuts its image in the water three times. Hence the name. Some translations say "Three Pools"—The Chinese character 潭 literally means "pool," but really there are no separate pools. There are three stone mini-pagodas that were created some 800 years ago, and during the Autumn full moon, a candle is lit inside each one to echo and enhance the moon's romantic glow. (One may see something like these in a temple; that would be a burner, empty inside, where worshipers can burn paper money for their relative's ghosts in the other world.)

Let's now get back to the story. The snake genie and Xu lived peacefully without further trouble until their son was born. Since the leaf of the wonderful herb was swallowed, the baby assumed the full human form like its father. But the snake genie had no milk, because snakes can only bear eggs; they don't have breasts for milk. Therefore, they employed a wet nurse to feed and look after the baby.

One day, a deplorable day, the monk Fahai came by. He said to Xu,

"Now it's time for me to catch the snake genie and send her to stay where she belongs."

Fahai took out a bowl. The magic bowl sucked the snake into it. Fahai carried the bowl and the snake to the Thunder-Peak Pagoda and put the snake under the pagoda so that she could not escape back into the human world. The green snake ran off to hide herself in the remote mountains where she and the white snake came from.

Xu found it best to raise his son like a normal boy, to avoid further trouble. He was a fine, intelligent boy. When he came of age, he passed the government examinations in the capital, and he was appointed an official. He was permitted to go home on a visit to his father. Then he learned what his mother was and where she was now. He went to the Thunder-Peak Pagoda and knelt before it. He cried and kowtowed, and cried and kowtowed till he shed bloody tears. Thus he touched the Heavenly Emperor, who made the pagoda collapse and the snake genie was able to escape back to where she came from.

CHAPTER 3. THE KARMA OF THREE SMILES

Tang Yin, a famous painter

Tang Yin (1470–1524) was a famous painter and poet in the Ming Dynasty (1368–1644). He wrote a poem in a special style, repeatedly using the words "flower" and "moon" in a way that evokes the very intoxication enjoyed on a bright night in the garden. It runs as follows:

"The Song of the Flowers and the Moon"

It's endless regret to have flowers without the moon,
but the regret is greater to have the moon without flowers.
The flower is lovely like a lady before the mirror of the moon,
The moonlight like the water shines over fragrant flowers.
Holding a candle under the moon I look for flowers,
And sipping wine, I taste it before flowers under the moon.
Such beautiful flowers and such a bright moon;
Don't take the moon and flowers as something ordinary.
The scent of flowers and the hue of the moon suit each other;
I sleep late being so fond of the moon and flowers.
The moon's setting and wine's gone down the throat, with
flowers before me;
though the flowers have faded, there's yet the moon urging
me to write poems.

Watching the moon through flowers, there's not much
shadow;
Watching the moon with flowers nearby in special beauty.
How many poets under the moon before flowers
Get drunk among flowers with the moon above every year?
The moon's overlooking the flowery path, shadows overlap;
Flowers so fragrant and beautiful with the moon so brilliant.
I sleep late being fond of the moon with flowers still in bloom;
I rise early to see flowers and the moon's just past zenith.
The shadow moving in the vast sky like flowers meeting the
moon;
I return to the deep courtyard, the moon accompanying
flowers.
I admire feelings between flowers and the moon in the hu-
man world;
I touch flowers and enjoy the moonlight, drunk with the
flowing afterglow.
The moon and flowers in Spring are worth a thousand taels
of gold;
I love the aroma of flowers and the shadow of the moon.
Flowers blow under the moon while Spring's silent and
lonely;
The moon moves above the tips of flowers while the night
is deep.
I hold the cup to invite the moon's shadow, tipsy before
flowers,
While my hands play with flower stems and chant a poem
facing the moon.
The moon wanes readily and flowers wither;
I must not lose heart but enjoy flowers under the moon.
Flowers in their beauty, full bloom, and the moon in great
brilliance;
I love the fragrance of flowers and the shadow of the moon.
The moonbeams come to the courtyard to shine on flowers,
While flowers follow moonbeams casting their shadows on
gauze windows.
Flowers may be defeated by the moon with full brilliance
And the moon may be lost to the flowers' scent all over the
path.

The moon and flowers become two beauties in the human
world;
To enjoy the moonlight beside flowers needs wine on credit.
A courtyard of flowers and the moonlight in springtime;
Flowers so fragrant and the moon so beautiful.
The wind sways flower stems to search for moon shadow;
Heaven opens the mirror of the moon to shine on the flower
fairies.
Slowly beat the flower drums in the moonlight;
The fife played under the moon sounds softly below flowers.
I'm afraid when flowers asleep and the moon setting,
The moon terrace and flower pavilion will be bleak.
The bright moon shines over flowers on high terrace;
I'm in reverie facing the moon and looking at flowers.
The moon's so round and flowers so good tonight;
But the moon was pale and the flowers were weak last year.
I hold up my cup to toast the moon and pour wine on flowers,
While I weave verses to comment on flowers and ask the
moon.
I'm thoroughly intoxicated and will sleep under the moon
and flowers,
Fearing the moon and flowers will laugh at me being an idiot.
Flowers blooming on a thousand stems and the moon like a
round wheel;
Heaven grants the moon and flowers to a free person,
Who may be the host of the moon or flowers,
Having just been the guest of the moon, then the guest of
flowers.
Flowers under the moon will detain me for a drink;
The moon before flowers won't detest my poverty.
How many good flowers are here, and how good is the moon!
How many people are enjoying the flowers and chanting un-
der the moon?
The moon turns toward the east wall and the flower shad-
ows so dark;
Flowers welcome the soul of the moon for its visage.
The emotional moon shines on the dew among flowers;
The understanding flowers swing in the wind under the moon.
Clouds break and the moon peeps at the beauty of flowers;

Flowers slumber in the deep night under the bright moon.
How many times in a human life can there be flowers and
   the moon
Such that the hue of the moon and the scent of flowers are
   the same everywhere?
When flowers are in full bloom, the moon is so bright;
Flowers resemble gauze and satin while the moon looks
   silvery.
In one sweeping moonbeam there are a thousand flowers;
Before the beautiful blossoming flowers there's a wheel of a
   moon.
How many thoughts do flowers have under the moon?
And how much spirit does the moon have among flowers?
Wait for the night when the moon sets and the flowers fade,
Which will sadden to death those who seek flowers and ask
   for the moon.
Flowers in spring and the moon in autumn suit each other;
The moon vies for brightness and the flowers for beauty.
When flowers blow in the moonlight, the aroma loads the
   trees;
The moonlight envelopes the flowers and the boughs' shad-
   ows intertwine.
The moon of the plum that falls in the dream of South of
   Yangtze River;
The sweet osmanthus flower in the moon conveys the Ci of
   Chengbei.*
How do flowers feel and what does the moon mean?
I will follow the moon and flowers to float the golden cup.

His father, Tang Jide, owned a wine house, so his was a well-
to-do family in Suzhou city. He had a brother, six years younger,
and a sister. In 1498, he took the local government test and came
out first among all the candidates. But he never wanted to be an
official and lived only as a painter. His paintings are collected
and stored in various museums in the world. His two paintings, "Picture of the Dream Deity — Weed Hall" and "Picture
of ChangE (the Chinese moon goddess)," are now in the Metro-
politan Museum of Art, New York.

---

* Name of a special kind of poetic style.

The legend of Tang Yin

The story of Tang is really a legend, popularly known by Chinese people and turned into movies and plays. It is a love story with a happy ending. In real life, Tang had three wives, but one after another. If one had three spouses at the same time, the first was wife and the other two were called concubines. In this legend Tang had eight wives already and the new one he found in the tale would be the ninth. So there was a book in Chinese titled "Nine Beauties" that was the narration of his love tale.

One warm spring day, Tang went to Tiger-Mound Temple in the outskirts of Suzhou city, which was a famous scenic spot. Besides tourists, there were many visitors who came to worship the Buddha in the temple. As the temple was renowned, many visitors came from other nearby cities. Tang went there just to enjoy the scene. He walked alongside a river, until he reached a spot where he saw a big ship anchoring at the riverside. There were two palanquins, one big and the other small, on the bank. Then a girl, who looked like a maid, to judge from her dress, was helping an elderly lady walk down the gang plank. The old lady got into the big palanquin and the maid into the small one. The carriers shouldered the palanquins and conveyed them toward the temple at some distance, followed by servants in uniforms. The lady must come from a rich, or even an official family.

The maid was very beautiful. Tang always fell for beautiful girls, no matter whether she came from a rich or poor family, so he followed them to the temple, where he had originally intended to go. The two palanquins were set down at the gate of the temple. The old lady got out and so did the maid. The lady walked in, closely followed by the maid. The servants walked a few steps behind. The lady entered the main hall where the huge statue of Buddha sat. All along the walls on both sides there were statuettes of arhans in various postures. In front of the statue there was a big, long table on which lay rows of candlesticks. Before the long table there was a bronze incense burner, where worshipers could put in the burned joss-sticks. The burned candles went onto the candlesticks. A little away from the incense burner there were three mats for worshipers to kneel on.

First, the lady got to her knees on one mat, kowtowing three times. When she got up on her feet, she walked round to look at the arhan statuettes. Then the maid knelt on one mat and at the same time, Tang went to kneel on the mat next to her, purposely letting one of his knees rest on the corner of her skirt. The maid kowtowed three times and wanted to stand up, but she could not, as her skirt was under the knee of a stranger beside her. She just smiled (the first smile, as Tang counted) at him as if to say, "You've caught my skirt under your knee." Tang got up quickly, saying, "Sorry!" The maid got up too, and walked to the side of the lady. He followed a couple of steps behind her, everywhere she went in the temple. He even followed her to the riverside and watched them get on board the ship.

Tang knew that they did not come from Suzhou city but from somewhere else. He walked alongside the bank, looking for a boat that he could ride in and follow the ship to where it came from. Luckily, he soon found a boat and he asked the boatman for a ride, promising to pay him extra. He asked the boatman to follow the ship wherever it sailed. The boatman was curious why the man wanted him to follow the ship, but it was none his business as long as he got paid.

Many boatmen around Suzhou city liked to sing and improvise songs. Tang asked him to sing some song of courtship and promised to pay for every song he sang. So the boatman sang something about lovemaking. Tang hoped that when the maid heard it, she would come out of the cabin to have a look, and then he could see her once more. But to his disappointment, the girl was not so curious. She never made her appearance.

Nightfall came and the ship anchored by the riverside for the night. The boat anchored at a little distance behind the ship. Nothing happened during the night. Early in the morning, Tang stood on the bow of the boat, watch the sunrise. Suddenly, the cabin door opened on the ship and the maid came out, carrying a basin of dirty water the old lady had used to wash her face and hands. The maid went to the stern of the ship and poured the water into the river without looking down. The water poured all over Tang, who cried out loud as if surprised that such thing could happen to him. He was just flaring up when he saw the maid looking down from the stern—she heard the cry and did not know what it was for. So she leaned out to have a look.

Then she saw the man, who had followed her here, wet through and his cap askew by water poured on it. She could not help but smile (the second smile as Tang counted) at him as if to say sorry. His anger was gone as he saw the beauty. Then the maid retired to the cabin.

The ship sailed again and the boat followed closely. In the late afternoon the ship reached its destination, Dongting town. Tang got ashore. Presently the lady and her maid appeared. Their residence was close to the river. The gate opened to welcome the lady's return. She and her maid walked to the gate. When the girl walked by Tang, somehow, she smiled again to him. (The third smile during Tang's courtship.) The girl went out of his sight. Tang stood there motionless as if enchanted by magic. Tang took the three smiles as a sign of love: the girl loved him. But in reality, the girl had smiled at him simply because he was acting so oddly.

Tang disguised as a servant

This was the manor in which resided a retired high-rank official by the surname of Hua. The old lady was his wife, the mistress of the household. They had two sons, but neither one was intelligent. In fact, they were both slow-witted. But both were married. The parents of two girls had allowed their daughters to marry such fools because the Hua family was wealthy and held a high social status. The wife of the second son was a cousin of Tang. The residence had a big garden in the back, with a small pond and grottoes, pavilions and arbors here and there. It was modeled on the customary plan for an old manor in the Ming Dynasty.

His Excellency Hua was the master of the household and father of the two idiots. He found a tutor and asked the old scholar to stay in the manor to teach his sons how to read and write. But the sons made little progress in studies for quite a few years. The tutor felt ashamed of himself for not being able to get better results.

Tang stood there at a loss, facing the closed gate, forgetting to pay the boatman. The boatman came ashore too, to remind Tang of his payment. Tang suddenly realized that he had left home without taking any money with him. What could he do now? He could not refuse to pay the boatman, which would damage his reputation as a famous painter. Then he realized that he had a folding fan with him, and that he had painted some flowers on it. His paintings at that time were worth considerable money. He gave the fan to the boatman as his fare. When the boatman returned to Suzhou city, he simply went to a pawn shop and traded the fan for money. The owner of the shop checked the fan for what it was worth. When he found that the picture was drawn by Tang Yin, he knew that it was worth a lot of money, but he gave the boatman only twenty taels. The boatman was happy to get so much money for a fan. He would never know that he was cheated by the owner.

Tang was trying to think of a way to get into the manor so that he would have more chances to see the beauty. The old lady had four handmaids, called Spring Scent, Summer Scent, Autumn Scent and Winter Scent. The beautiful maid was Autumn Scent. The other three were just so-so. The lady liked Autumn Scent the most. She had learned to read and write a little, and could also draw pictures, while the other three were illiterate.

All at once, a wonderful idea struck Tang. He sold his good-quality clothes and got some shabby clothes. He put on the old clothes and lay down in front of the gate. He cried bitterly and loudly, so that the gatekeeper inside the gate could hear him. In the olden days, every Chinese manor house had a gatekeeper to open and shut the gate. Just inside the house, there was a room for the gatekeeper to sleep in. He stayed in that room all day and all night.

This was a kind man with a heart of gold. He would easily sympathize with the poor and those in need. When he heard the bitter cry, he opened a small door by the gate and came out to see what was the matter. Then he saw a young man in shabby clothes, crying. He asked what was wrong. Tang replied that he had come here to look for his uncle, but the uncle had died and now he had no money and did not know where to go and how to keep his body and soul together. The old janitor sympathized with him. He said to Tang that the master of this house was looking to hire another servant for wait on his two sons, and if he did not mind taking the job, he would report to the master.

Tang accepted the offer immediately. Therefore, the janitor went in to report to the master, who sent for Tang to be brought into his presence.

After learning of Tang's sad experience, His Excellency Hua asked Tang his name. As the name Tang Yin was known to almost everyone in the province, he had to invent a false one. So he gave his name as Kang Xuan, which in Chinese characters looked somewhat alike. But in such a big house, all the servants had to change their original names to whatever name the master gave; so Tang was called Hua An. Every servant had to use the family's last name Hua. But the maids and woman servants did not have to use the last name.

It was a routine for new servants to kowtow to the elderly lady and the wives of the sons. Therefore, he first went to see the lady and kowtowed before her without any problem. Then he went to kowtow to the wife of the elder son, led there by the maid Spring Scent, without problem either. But when he had to see the wife of the younger son and kowtow to her, he felt awkward because she was his cousin and she would surely recognize him. When his real identity was revealed, he would be driven out of the household. And he could not avoid it. He had to follow the maid there. He walked slowly, hoping to delay the meeting. But the maid urged him along. He thought that if he would not let his cousin see his face, she would not recognize him. As soon as he stepped into his cousin's room, he got on his knees at once with his face downward towards the floor. The maid said that he must go closer to the wife and kowtow right in front of her. So he crawled closer and kowtowed. So far so good, but this woman was smart. He had to say a few words in greeting, and his voice betrayed him. His cousin immediately became aware that this was her cousin and he had come for a girl.

She understood immediately that the girl he loved must be Autumn Scent, as she was the most beautiful person in this household. None of the other girls were worth his efforts to disguise himself as a servant. She would not reveal his true identity, but she would blackmail him. She had always wanted him to paint for her a painting of Bodhisattva so that she could hang it on the wall and worship it every day. It would also be worth a lot of money. Tang was lazy about painting anything as a gift to anyone, and that's why his cousin wanted to take this chance to blackmail him. He could refuse it this time.

As Hua An (Tang) could read and write, he was assigned to work in the study where the tutor taught the sons, like a classroom. Hua An would prepare tea for the tutor and the sons, and he would go to the kitchen to bring them lunch. After classes, in late afternoon, the two sons would go to their living quarters in the back of the manor house and the tutor would retire to his own room. Tang cleaned up the study and that was all the work for him.

Once when Tang went to the kitchen for some hot water to make tea for the tutor and the sons, unexpectedly he met Autumn Scent there, who had come to ask the cook for some snacks for the old lady. That was just what Tang wanted. He stepped forward to say hello to her, but she ignored him. She recognized him, but did not know why he had come to work as a servant or what he wanted of her. She just took refreshments and returned to the room where the lady was waiting. Afterwards, Tang met Autumn Scent a few times, but he could never get a word with her.

Tang promoted to Tutor

As the sons had not made any progress in their studies, the old tutor felt ashamed of himself and decided that he was too old for teaching, so he resigned and left the household. His Excellency Hua sought for some other tutors for his sons, but no one would come to teach such idiots. Finally the father thought of Tang, as he had demonstrated his rich knowledge of the language, and he let Tang teach his sons. Tang no longer had to debase himself by working as a servant.

Another day, after class, Tang met Autumn Scent in the garden. Here was the chance to express his love for her, and so he would not let her go. He told her everything about himself and even produced his personal seal to prove that he really was the one with his name engraved on the seal: Tang Yin. He asked her to marry him and promised she would live happily ever after. Autumn Scent believed him, but she could not make any promise to marry him. She had to ask the permission of the old lady.

She said she could meet him at night, after her mistress was asleep, at the Peony Arbor in the garden to talk over the matter. Then they went different ways.

Autumn Scent came across the elder son, who liked her very much and had always wanted her to be his concubine. He would not let her go and wanted her to promise to marry him. She was disgusted with him and so wanted to play a trick on him. She promised to meet him at night at the Peony Arbor, but earlier than Tang would come. After she left the elder son behind, she met the younger son, who liked her too and wanted her to be his concubine, too. She promised to meet him at the same time and the same place as the other son.

At the time of appointment that night, the two sons came to the arbor. They were surprised to see each other. The elder son asked the younger son why he had come there. The latter replied that he came to look at the moon, so bright. And he also asked his brother the same question. His brother answered that he was there for the same purpose. But they both knew what the real reason was.

Before long, their mother came, accompanied by Autumn Scent, the maid. The maid walked ahead with a lantern to lead the way, followed by the old lady. The two sons saw the maid and did not spy their mother. They stepped forward to flirt with the maid, who stepped aside. Then they saw their mother, who quickly grasped the situation. She was infuriated and scolded the sons and bade them to go away, right off. The sons ran away as fast as their legs could carry them. At that moment, Tang arrived, but when he saw the old lady, he hid himself behind a grotto. The lady went back to her own room, followed by Autumn Scent. Tang had lost this chance. He wished that he could have persuaded Autumn Scent to elope with him. Surely, he could find another opportunity for it.

Tang marries Autumn Scent

The two sons made some progress in their studies under Tang's instruction. The old tutor was not lacking in learning, but that he did not have a good method to such pupils as these. Tang knew how to teach them. He taught them how to write

couplets first, little by little. He taught them how to pair mountain with river. Then to add some other words, like stands and
flows, to make complete sentences. Mountain stands against
river flows. Then add more words, like high and fast. Thus, they
had the couplet as Mountain stands high, River flows fast. The
father was glad that his sons could at least write couplets now.
He depended on Tang to make his sons better off in their studies.

Tang had stayed here already several months. His wives at
home had not seen him for so long that they began to fear that
something had happened to him. They did not even know if he
was still alive or already dead. Then they invited his best friend
Zhu Zhishan and asked him if he knew where their husband
was now. However, he had no idea at all. He was looking for
him, too. As best friends, they often met each other. Now Tang
was nowhere to be found; he had evaporated into the thin air.
Zhu Zhishan promised the wives to do his utmost to find their
husband as soon as he could.

Zhu thought that Tang might have left Suzhou for somewhere else. He often followed his eccentric disposition and
could take off to distant parts without notice, vanishing from
the face of the earth, and after many months he would reappear
just as suddenly. If he had gone somewhere, he must have taken
a boat, reasoned his friend. Boats were the main transportation
in Suzhou. Therefore, he went to the riverside to ask the boatmen, one by one, till he found the boatman who had taken Tang
to Dongting town. Zhu knew that this must have something
to do with girls, as usual. He asked the boatman to take him to
where he had dropped off Tang.

Finally he stepped ashore when the boat anchored. He
learned that it was the residence of His Excellency Hua, in
whose manor house there must be many beautiful girls. Tang
must have come in pursuit of one of them. As Zhu was also a famous scholar, and a calligrapher as well, if he wanted to visit his
Excellency, he would certainly be invited in, though he and the
host had not met each other before. So he sent his hand-written
name card and was soon invited to go into the waiting room. He
seated himself in the reception room and waited for the host to
make his appearance.

Presently, Hua came in and they greeted each other and both

sat down. After they chatted for a few minutes, Zhu started to write one sentence of a couplet and asked Hua to write another sentence to complete the couplet. That was a common activity in intellectual circles. But Hua was not versed in such things and got the idea of letting Tang come out to write it for him. So Tang came to meet the guest. They recognized each other, but acted as if they were strangers. Then Zhu began to take his leave and asked Tang to see him out. Mr. Hua agreed. So Tang followed Zhu to the riverside and they talked. Tang told Zhu why he was staying here, and now there was no way for him to get the girl. He needed some new idea. Zhu could always get wonderful ideas for his friends. So they bade each other farewell, for now.

Tang went back to the manor house to see Hua, the master, and reported to him that he had seen the guest off at the riverside. He added that he would like to resign and go to work for Zhu. Hua demanded to know the reason, so Tang answered that Zhu was willing to give him one of his maids to be his wife, besides his pay. Hua was angry, saying, "You can stay here and continue to teach my sons! I will give one of our maids to be your wife." Tang said, "The guest said that he would let me choose one of his maids according to my taste, not just give me one." Hua said, "I will let you choose one, too." Tang was happy and promised to stay.

Then Hua notified his lady of the decision. The lady had no objection; it was important that the sons were finally learning something and overcoming their disgrace. They selected a red-letter day and in the evening, all the young maids were gathered together in the sitting room. Some of the maids knew clearly that they were just plain and would have no chance to be chosen. Other maids held the hope of being selected, as they also liked the handsome servant (now half servant, half tutor). They were attired as best they knew how.

When Tang came in, all eyes centered on his face. Just as all young men love to see beautiful girls, girls love to see handsome young men. Beauty always attracts attention. Tang stood in front of two rows of girls and looked at every face to find the one he loved. But the one he loved was not among the girls. The mistress of the house was not so foolish as to have her favorite maid be chosen and leave her alone. So the master sat by the table at the end of the sitting room with rows of girls on his right side and Tang on his left.

As Tang did not make his selection, the master asked him whom he would choose. Tang just shook his head, which meant that none among the maids were to his liking. Hua asked his steward if everyone was here. The steward looked at all the girls and found that Autumn Scent was not present. So he replied that Autumn Scent had not arrived yet. The master sent the steward to fetch her. Now the old lady could not detain her favorite maid anymore. When Autumn Scent made her appearance in the room, Tang immediately said that he would choose Autumn Scent.

Therefore, a new bedroom was prepared for the newly-wed couple. They had a wedding ceremony just among the household. Every fellow servant and woman servant congratulated them. At night, on the bed, Tang told Autumn Scent everything about him and they planned the elopement. Three days later, at midnight, they stole out of the manor house through the back door. Tang had rented a boat and it was waiting for them by the riverside. Once they were on board, the boat rowed away to Suzhou city.

Next day, both the bride and the bridegroom were expected to begin to work after their wedding vacation.

But they never appeared, even at lunch time. The steward went to knock at their room. No response. So he broke into the room and found no one was there. The couple were nowhere to be found. They had just disappeared. The steward went to report to the master. The master was bewildered as to why they had disappeared. He sent all the manservants to seek for them in the neighborhood, but in vain. They were long gone to Suzhou city.

Hua did not have any idea who Tang was. He sent his steward to go to Suzhou city to see Zhu and asked him who was Tang and where they could find him. Frankly, Zhu told the steward that it was Tang Yin, and then let the steward know the whole story. The steward went back to report to his master. Meanwhile, Zhu notified Tang, who at once sent someone to the manor house with one of his best paintings.

When Hua got this report from the steward, he was furious

and wanted to sue Tang, but soon after, he received the gift. He had always admired Tang's paintings. Now he had gotten one, and he was satisfied. He forgave Tang. The old lady, though fond of her favorite maid, was also glad to know that she had married a famous painter. The lady had always worried who would have her favorite maid as wife. Who could be worth such a beauty for his wife? She would never let any of the menservants marry her. Now she had got a husband worthy of her. The old lady declared that the maid was her adopted daughter and sent her a dowry. Sometime later, Autumn Scent and her husband came to visit her adoptive father and mother. Everyone was happy. The couple lived happily ever after.

CHAPTER 4. THE TALE OF LIANG AND ZHU

Changing appearances

Back in the Eastern Jin Dynasty (317–420 AD), a boy named Liang Shanbo lived in Guiji town and a girl named Zhu Yingtai lived in Shangyu town, both in Zhejiang province. There was a good government-run school in Hangzhou city, the capital of the province. Education at a local school began when boys were five or six. Girls from rich families had private tutors coming to teach them at home. Boys of poor families had to help their parents work for a living and had no chance to study, let alone girls. When boys of wealthy families reached the age of twenty, they were allowed to go to Hangzhou city for further education in the government-run school.

One day, Liang left home for Hangzhou city and was on the way there, followed by his page Sijiu, who carried luggage for both of them. From another direction came Zhu, from Shangyu town, disguised as a boy, with her maid disguised as a page. She was a girl who liked to do everything at her own free will, and she had more freedom as a boy. Her parents always doted on her. As her parents had no son, the girl often dressed herself as a boy to please her parents. And everyone was happy.

When she turned eighteen, she suddenly thought it would

be a fine idea to go to Hangzhou city and pursue further studies like the boys. Her parents could not dissuade her and had to let her go. So she attired her handmaid Yinxin, sixteen, as a page, and made the reparations. Since the maid could not carry much luggage, they decided to buy all the necessary things in Hangzhou city.

When they reached the thoroughfare to Hangzhou city, they saw a boy and his page walking in front them. Travel at that time was mostly by foot—especially since it was not far from to Hangzhou city. All the way, Zhu and her maid were telling jokes and laughing. Now their laughter came to the ears of the boy and his page. They turned round and looked to see who were laughing so merrily. When Liang found it was another boy and his page, he was glad to have company. Therefore, he stopped and waited for them to catch up. Zhu had the same thought.

As Zhu came close enough, Liang greeted her by raising his hands in front of his chest, the right hand wrapping on the left fist, and accosted her, "May I ask what is your surname?" Zhu replies, "My humble surname is Zhu." Lilang said, "Brother Zhu, where are you going?" Zhu said, "I'm going to Hangzhou city for education in the government-run school." Liang said joyfully, "So am I. Let's go together so that we can have company all the way there." Zhu agreed and then she asked, "May I have your surname?" Liang replied, "This is Liang."

They walked side by side with their pages walking side by side behind them. They chatted pleasantly. They became best friends, and then they became sworn brothers by vowing to heaven and earth on their knees that they would never betray each other, whatever happened. It was an old Chinese tradition. But all through Chinese history, there were cases when some sworn brothers did betray each other.

One day at last, they reached Hangzhou city and reported to school. The teachers there were all learned scholars. In the classroom, every student was assigned a small desk and chair. There were no blackboards yet, as they hadn't been invented. The teacher sat behind a big desk and the books he taught from were all classics. The lessons were primarily about language and literacy. No mathematics, no geography, no chemistry, nothing more. And if a student made mistakes, or offenses, the teacher could spank his hand on the palm with a ruler.

There was dorm where students lived and food was provided, too, but it was all paid for by the students' families. So most students were from rich families. Only a young genius could be accepted and receive free room and board, because the government needed geniuses to serve it. Generally two persons had a bedroom, the student and his page. The page could not listen to the lessons taught in the classroom. His duties were to look after the student, his master. Some diligent pages could listen outside the windows, which was not against the regulations.

The desks of Liang and Zhu were put side by side so that they could sometimes whisper to each other in class. They even told jokes about an old teacher with a goatee, who looked like a goat. The teacher was short-sighted and could not see what the students were doing at their desks.

They were also taught to practice calligraphy skills, by first imitating the writings of famous scholars in the previous generations. They learned how to use the Chinese writing brush, which was invented by Meng Tian (d. 210 BC.) He was a general serving the first emperor of the Qin Dynasty (221–207 BC). He guarded the north frontier and drove the minority people that often invaded Qin territory further north. He built part of the Great Wall.

Before the brush was invented, Chinese people used a knife to carve characters (words) on sticks of bamboo. They made a small hole on each stick of bamboo and used a long thin piece of leather to string together the bamboo pieces, and thus a book was made, the earliest book in China. When the brush was invented, people at first wrote on silk. Then when paper was invented, during the Han dynasty (206 BC–AD 220), people could write or paint on both silk and paper.

Liang and Zhu stuck together almost every day. So did their pages, but after all, pages should follow their masters everywhere the masters went. Once a fellow student suddenly found that there were tiny holes on Zhu's earlobes, which suggested that Zhu was a girl in disguise, because only girls would have holes in their earlobes. Now Zhu was embarrassed and soon she came up with an excuse, saying that she had always been sickly and a fortune-teller had advised her parents that she should have holes in her earlobes to prolong her life, or she would die soon. Those being superstitious times, her parents did as they were told by the fortune-teller. The excuse was somewhat lame, but her follow students could not say anything more about it.

They lived in Hangzhou for three years. One day, Zhu received a letter from her father, urging her to go home as her mother was ill. Zhu decided to leave the next day. Liang went with her, to see her off. They walked and chatted, reluctant to part, forgetful of how much distance they had covered.

Zhu said, "Brother Liang, I have a twin sister, looking very much like me. I want Brother Liang to marry her. What do you think?"

Liang said, "I think your twin sister must be lovely. I'd be very lucky if I could marry your sister. Would your parents agree?"

Zhu said, "As soon as you get home, you must tell your parents to send us a matchmaker. I'll try to persuade my parents."

At last, Zhu insisted that Liang should return to the school. Before separating, Zhu wanted Liang to promise to come to see her when he finished school and returned home. Liang promised and said that he would surely do it. Then they exchanged addresses. Zhu made her way home with her maid. Liang stood there, watching Zhu till she was no longer to be seen.

Another year elapsed and Liang finished his education. Now he had to go home. The page collected their things and they left the next day. During this year, Liang was always thinking of Zhu. Now he would have to go a little bit out of his way to visit his classmate first to make sure that Zhu's sister would marry him. Then he would hurry home and ask his parents to send a matchmaker.

He asked the way to where Zhu lived. After a few days, he at length found her house. He asked to see Zhu. A servant went in to contact the handmaid, informing her of Liang's visit. The maid ran to Zhu to ask what she should tell him. Zhu told the maid to invite Liang to come in and sit in the living room for a moment, and she hurriedly dressed to receive him. So Liang was let in and took his seat in the living room.

Presently, Zhu came in, and Liang was astonished to find a girl all dressed up. He thought that it must be the twin sister, but then where was the original Zhu, her brother? Zhu said to Liang,

"Brother Liang, it's me, your classmate and sworn brother Zhu."

Liang was bewildered. Then Zhu explained everything to him, adding that she had no twin sister. Liang was happy that he could have such an intelligent and beautiful girl for his wife. They had a heart-to-heart talk and recalled the joyful days at school. Then it was time for Liang to leave. Zhu saw Liang to the gate and at parting, Zhu reminded Liang to ask his parents to send a matchmaker as soon as possible.

The Butterfly Legend

Zhu waited and waited for the matchmaker to propose their marriage to her parents, but no one came. Meanwhile, many other matchmakers came, one after another. Boys in the neighborhood all knew that the daughter of the Zhu family was intelligent and beautiful. Every boy dreamed to have her for his wife. But after the parents learned the conditions of every boy in the neighborhood, they refused to give the hand of their daughter away to any of them. However, Liang's matchmaker never came. The girl was tearful and sorrowful. She was afraid that her parents would give her in marriage to another boy before Liang's matchmaker arrived.

When Liang got back home, he was suddenly taken ill and had no chance to talk to his parents about this. That was why no matchmaker was sent to Zhu's family. In ancient China, the marriage of sons and daughters were arranged by parents. The sons and daughters had no say in their own matter. If they married a good spouse, they were lucky. If they married a bad spouse, they were unlucky. That was their fate.

One day, another matchmaker came to see Zhu's parents. All the matchmakers were old women, and this is what they did for a living. This matchmaker was sent here by the district magistrate. His son had a good reputation and was also a diligent student. Therefore, Zhu's parents were glad to have such a future son-in-law. They consented to the marriage. They arranged a day to send the dowry and a day when the bridegroom would come to fetch his bride home. There was some distance between Zhu's family and the residence of the magistrate. The wedding would be a red-letter day (in the Chinese sense, referring to celebratory occasions when red envelopes with monetary gifts would be given), ten days later. When the maid learned the news, she went to tell Zhu. Zhu cried so bitterly that she became sick. So the wedding had to be postponed till the bride was recovered.

When Liang's page finally heard the sad news, he told Liang about it and Liang's sickness worsened. Not long afterwards, he died. His tomb was built somewhere along a thoroughfare in accordance with his will, so that the passengers could see that there lay a young man called Liang Shanbo, and so that his name would be known posthumously.

After the death of his master, the page secretly went to Zhu's house and found the maid. He told her about the death of his master Liang. The maid informed her mistress, who promptly made her life's decision.

As soon as the bride was recovered, the bridegroom came with a palanquin to take her home for the wedding ceremony. Before she left her family's house, the bride insisted that she must make a short detour to the grave of her former classmate to bid him farewell, though he was dead. His soul would know it, and he would bless her for her marriage. She really wanted his blessings. The bridegroom agreed, as he thought that it would do no harm for his bride to visit the tomb of a dead classmate. The procession marched towards the home of the bridegroom and stopped at the tomb of the classmate. The bride got out of the palanquin and walked over to salute the dead. Just as she stood in front of the tomb, the tomb exploded and made a big hole in the front part. The girl jumped in and a short while later, two huge, beautiful butterflies flew out of the tomb and hovered in midair. It was said that the souls of Liang and Zhu turned into butterflies.

CHAPTER 5. TALE OF THE WEST CHAMBER

Lodging in Pujiu Temple

Zhang Gong, a young man, was on his way to the capital to take part in the government test. If he passed, he could be appointed an official. His father had been a high official, but he died when Zhang Gong was a little boy. A few years later his mother died, too. Now he was alone and went to the capital. One evening, he came to the Pujiu Temple in Shanxi province (which now is open to visitors). In ancient China, every traveler could ask to lodge in a temple or someone's house without the need to pay, if there were no inns nearby. That was the tradition. The head monk, Facong, received him and let him stay in a guest room—the West Chamber.

At the same time, a family named Cui was also lodged here. The master of the Cui family had been a high official in the government. Now he had died and his family, the old lady and the daughter Cui Yingying, were taking his coffin back to bury in their home town. They went to the temple and stayed there. When the father was still alive, he had promised to marry his daughter to Zheng Heng, the son of a friend, when they both grew up. Nothing was put in writing; it was just an oral promise. Families often made such arrangements, and sometimes when the boy and the girl grew up, the parents were serious and married them together. But sometimes, people looked upon such notions as a joke told long ago and just laughed it off.

In China, most people were superstitious. When anyone died in the house, they would ask some monks or Taoists to come to chant a sutra to bless the ghost and they hoped that by the chanting of the Buddhist sutra the ghost could be quickly born into its next life. Since the Cui family was now in a temple, the old lady asked the monks there to perform the ritual for a few days.

When Zhang arrived, the ritual was under way in a large hall. The lady and her daughter were sitting aside to watch the ritual going on. Zhang wanted to go in to have a look, but the head monk stopped him, saying, "It is a private family service. No intrusion from outsiders." Anyway, Zhang had a glimpse of the daughter, so beautiful. The young man immediately fell in love with her.

The Cui family lived in the back garden of the temple. The West Chamber was separated from the back garden by a low wall. One could look at the garden over the low wall. Every night Yingying, the daughter would go into the garden to burn incense for her deceased father. On the very night Zhang moved in, he walked to the wall and looked at the girl while he recited a poem of his own composition to sing the girl's praises. When she heard it, she also read aloud a poem to respond to his. A girl always liked a poet. It was a Chinese tradition for a boy and a girl to recite poems to each other to express their love.

Promise of marriage

On a nearby mountain lived a group of outlaws. The leader was called Flying Tiger. When he was told that a beautiful girl had come to stay in the temple, he went there to demand that he should take the girl away to be his wife. He gave a three-day time limit. If at the end of three days, the girl did not come out, he would break into the temple and take her away by force. When the lady and the daughter were informed of this, they were so frightened that the lady declared whoever could save them from this disaster, she would let him marry her daughter. She thought that it would be better for her daughter to marry someone who was capable of saving them than to allow the daughter to be kidnapped by outlaws.

Was it a coincidence or destiny that young Zhang's best friend, Du Que, was a general guarding a nearby city? He wrote a letter and asked the monk to slip out the back of the temple and get the letter to his friend Du. Once Du read his letter, he would come to their rescue right away. It was a day's journey from the temple to the city. So Du hastened over the next day with his soldiers and drove the outlaws away.

Then the friends greeted each other and Zhang thanked Du profusely. After a few hours' reunion, Du had to go back to his duties to guard the city. He could not be absent too long. But he had left behind some soldiers to defend the temple lest the outlaws showed up while he was gone.

The crisis was over now. But the lady did not want to keep her promise to let Zhang marry her daughter. She wanted to stick to the promise her deceased husband had given to a friend of his. But the daughter did not love the son of her father's friend, as he was not a poet. She loved this young man, the young poet, for she could write poems herself.

That night, under the bright moon, Zhang conveyed his lovesickness by playing the zither and the girl also played the zither in response, just like young men in old Spain, playing guitar under the window or balcony of the girls they loved. However, the mother forbade Zhang to see the girl. He was heartsick and fell ill. The girl learned of this and sent her maid Hongniang to see how the young man was faring.

Then Zhang wrote a love letter and asked the maid to take it to the girl. She wrote a letter in return, and the maid became their messenger. The girl wrote to ask Zhang to come out to see her in the moonlight. At the night of the appointment, the girl played her zither in the back garden. When Zhang heard the zither sound, he came to the low wall to look at the girl. Then he climbed over the wall and met the girl face to face. They vowed to love each other forever and ever.

Happy ending

The lady noticed that her daughter was acting oddly and she summoned the maid to speak to her. She wanted the maid to tell her what was happening between her daughter and the young man, and she insisted that she wanted to know the truth. She threatened that if the maid did not tell the truth, she would be spanked. The maid had nothing to do but had to tell the lady what had taken place between her mistress and the young man up to this point. Then she begged the lady to let her mistress marry the one she loved, or the daughter might die of lovesickness. The lady knew her daughter well, and after serious consideration, consented that the daughter could marry the young man on one condition. He must pass the government tests and become an official before he could marry her daughter.

This good news helped the young man recover very quickly. Now, the daughter was happy too. She held a dinner party to bid farewell to the young man, demanding him not to transfer his love to other girls while he was in the capital to become an official. A few days later, the young man started on his way. Every night he lodged in an inn and every night he dreamed of the girl.

Zhang did pass the government tests and he was appointed the mayor of Hezhong city. He wrote a letter to the girl to report the good news. While the letter was en route, the other young man, Zheng Heng, who was supposed to be the girl's husband as promised by her father, came to see her, intending to marry her. When he learned the situation, he decided to tell a lie: that Zhang had married the daughter of the premier. The lady, who still wanted to marry her daughter to the son of her husband's friend, decided to marry her daughter right off, now, in the temple, on the pretense that Zhang would never be back. The girl cried, but she could not disobey her mother. So a date was set.

On the very day the wedding ceremony was to take place, the letter from Zhang arrived. The very next day Zhang himself came, because he had to reach the city where he was to be mayor in just a few days. He made a short detour to marry his bride and take her to the city he would administer. Seeing that his trick had failed, and he was now exposed as a liar, Zheng Heng could only withdraw. So the wedding ceremony took place as prepared. Only the bridegroom was changed. After the marriage, the lady and her daughter went with the young man to live in the city, and the couple lived happily ever after.

CHAPTER 6. THE TUNE OF THE PHOENIX COURTING

There was a rich family named Zhuo in Linqiong town, Sichuan province. The father was Zhuo Wangsun and his only daughter was Zhuo Wenjun. She was married at the age of sixteen, but her husband soon died. After a couple of years, she returned to her father's home. Wenjun was still beautiful and was quite talented. She could play music and write poetry.

Here are four of her rondeau-like poems. In Chinese, many parts of a sentence may be left out if they can be inferred, and that includes the subject of the sentence, pronouns, and articles like "the."

1) Spring
> Orioles chirp, bank willows play in fine spring;
> Willows play in fine spring, bright moon at night.
> Bright moon at night, fine spring plays with willows
> Fine spring plays with willows on bank with chirping orioles.

2) Summer
> Fragrant lotus, green water moving, wind so cool;
> Water moving, wind cool, summer day so long.
> Long day, summer so cool, wind moving water;
> Cool wind moving water, green lotus fragrant.

3) Autumn

> At autumn river, Chu* wild geese sleeping on sand shoal;
> Wild geese sleeping on sand shoal, shallow water flows.
> Flowing water, shallow shoal of sand with sleeping wild geese;
> Shoal of sand with sleeping wild geese, Chu river in autumn.

4) Winter

> Red burner, permeating charcoal heating cold wind;
> Charcoal heating cold wind to defy freezing winter.
> In winter so freezing, to defy wind of cold with heating charcoal;
> In wind so cold, heat of charcoal permeates the burner red.

Suma Xiangru (179–117 BC) was a famous man of letters and great essayist of West Han dynasty (206 BC–8 AD), but he was destitute. (He had a double surname; there are quite a few double surnames made of two words in the list of Chinese surnames.) He liked to travel, and one day he arrived in Linqiong town at the invitation of his friend Wang Ji, the mayor of the town.

Zhuo Wangsun, living alone except for his daughter, decided to liven things up and so he held a banquet, inviting the mayor and his friend Suma, too, as the talented man was so renowned that the host and many of the guests had heard of him. They all asked him to play a tune. Suma gladly agreed. He always carried his zither with him, a famous zither that had a popular name of Luuqi. He sang while he played to the tune of "Male Phoenix Seeking a Female," which ran as follows:

> There's a beauty, wow,
> None can forget once seen.
> If I don't see her for a day, oh,
> I'll go mad thinking of her.
> Like a male phoenix flying far and wide, oh,
> Seeking a female one over the four seas.
> What can I do, since the beauty, oh,

---

* Chu is the name of an ancient state, now generally denoting the area to south of the Yangtze River.

Is not within the eastern wall.
I use a zither instead of words, oh,
To express my deep love for her.
When can she agree to marry me, oh,
To console me in my restlessness.
But they say she'll marry a man of virtue, oh,
And go with him hand in hand.
Then I can't fly with her like a pair of phoenix, oh,
I'm so downhearted I could die.

The banquet hall had two doors, the front one for guests, and the back one, which the servants used when carrying dishes—but there was a big, long screen shielding the back door so that the guests could not see it. The servants had to go round the screen to get to the tables serving food.

Mr. Zhuo's widowed daughter Wenjun was told that the famous essayist would be attending, and so she stood behind the screen to listen to what was going on. Suma knew that the Zhuo family had a beautiful daughter who had recently been widowed. By the song he sang, he hoped to convey his admiration and love for her. The daughter understood the message through the song, and she also admired the famous essayist. So at night, she collected her belongings and went to see Suma at his lodging place. Thus, they eloped together. That was a bold action for a woman in the ancient China.

Suma and Wenjun went back to Chengdu city (in the same province), where Suma came from. His home was just a small cabin with almost nothing inside. Wenjun's father was very angry when he was informed of the elopement. It was a shameful thing in ancient China. He decided not to give his daughter any money, to see how they could get on. The husband Suma could play zither beautifully and could write the best essays at the time, but he did not have any skills for making a living. Finally they decided to move back to Linqiong town and sold their cabin to make some money. When they got back, they opened a wine shop there. The wife served as a cashier behind the counter and the husband worked as a waiter, serving food and wine.

Some friends talked with the father, saying that Wenjun was his own flesh and blood. She was now leading a poor life.

A father had some responsibility for his daughter. Besides, she had married a famous man of letters, not just any poor bum. The son-in-law would have a bright future some day. Her father was at last persuaded and gave the daughter money. Then they lived better. They had a daughter named Qinxin, born on the first day of the first moon in the lunar calendar.

Suma was so well-known all over the country that his name reached the ear of the Emperor, who sent for Suma and made him a courtier in his court. While he was there, a favorite concubine of the Emperor heard Suma's name mentioned and she knew that he was the best writer. It happens that she had offended the Emperor and he had ignored her for some time. She sent a eunuch to see Suma and gave him money. She wanted him to write an article she could give to the Emperor. He wrote an essay that became famous and when the Emperor read it, he was so touched that he reconciled with the concubine.

When Suma was at the capital, his wife stayed behind in the town. Suma was now an official; and he came to know a girl. He wanted to have her as his concubine. He wrote a letter to his wife and said that he wanted to divorce her. When the wife received the letter, she was woeful and cried bitterly. She wrote a poem and sent it to her husband. The poem reads like this:

> My love for you is white as the snow on the mountain.
> My feeling for you is like the moon among the clouds.
> Now I know you have some other intention,
> And want to divorce me for the new one.
> Today I drink wine for you for the last time;
> Tomorrow we flow apart like water in a brook.
> I stroll by a clear creek coming out of the palace;
> The water in it flows east and west just like us.
> So melancholy and so sorrowful.
> No need to cry when being divorced.
> I wish to have a man with everlasting love,
> To live together till white hair grows.
> Why is the fishing rod trembling?
> The fish caught, its tail is shaking.
> A man should be loyal and faithful,
> Why change for money and pelf?

When Suma received the letter and the poem, he was greatly moved and gave up the idea of having a concubine. He let the wife come to the capital to live with him till their hair grew white on their heads.

CHAPTER 7. THE COWHERD AND THE WEAVER GIRL

At night in the sky, two bright stars can be seen. One is Vega (in Chinese mythology, it is known as the Weaver Girl). The other is Altair (in Chinese mythology, it is known as the Cowherd). The Cowherd and the girl weaver loved each other but had to keep it secret, because it was against the heavenly rules. At last their love was found out by the Mother Goddess, who was infuriated. Then the Mother Goddess ordered the Cowherd to go through incarnation to become a mortal. The Cowherd was born into a peasant family. As for the girl, she was punished by being set to weave clouds forever, without rest. From the loom, she wove out all sorts of clouds, in all shapes and all colors. The clouds are known in Chinese mythology as heavenly robes.

When the Cowherd grew up, his parents died. He had an elder brother who was married. The sister-in-law insisted on dividing the few things the parents had left to them, and the Cowherd got only an old cow. He used her to till a small piece of land and grew some rice and vegetables on it. He put up a shabby little hut and slept in it at night. Life was hard for him.

One day, all of a sudden, the old cow began to speak human language to the Cowherd. She said, "Cowherd, today, you must go to the Green-Lotus Pond. Goddesses are bathing in it. Steal the red robe and hide somewhere. Then you can have a wife."

The Cowherd was so surprised, he wasn't sure if he was just hearing things. The old cow insisted, "Go ahead and try it."

The Cowherd went there and hid himself behind bushes. Presently, some girls came along and took off their clothes and bathed in the pond. The girls wore clothes of different colors. The Cowherd crawled out to the edge of the pond without being noticed. He stealthily took the red robe and crawled back where he had hidden. Then after bathing, the girls put on their clothes and went away. But the girl who had worn the red robe could not find her clothes anywhere. If she could not find her clothing, how could she go back? She started to cry. At that moment, the Cowherd appeared from behind the bushes with the red robe. He said to the girl, "If you marry me, I'll give you the robe." (Sounds like blackmail?) The girl had to marry him, or she could never get out of the pond.

The Cowherd took her back to his hut. They worked hard. The Cowherd still grew rice and other plants. The girl wove cloth for the Cowherd to take to the market for sale. Soon they had two children.

One day the old cow was dying. Before her death, she told the Cowherd that when she died, he must cut off her two horns and that would help him some day. So the Cowherd did as he was told. And he buried the cow the way he had buried his parents.

Unluckily for them, the Mother Goddess learned of this and sent a messenger to take the Weaver Girl back to heaven. The messenger caught the girl by her hand and flew with her up towards heaven. The Cowherd took the two children and wanted to go after her, but he could not fly. Just at that time, the two cow horns he was carrying grew bigger and seemed about to take off. He and his two sons got on the horns and began to pursue the Weaver Girl.

The Mother Goddess watched from heaven and saw this. She took out her hairpin and drew a line between the Weaver Girl and the Cowherd and their sons. The line became a celestial river that separated them. In Chinese mythology the celestial river is the Milky Way. The sons yelped bitterly and the Weaver Girl besought the Mother Goddess to have mercy on them. So the Mother Goddess permitted them to meet once a year on the night of the seventh day of the seventh moon in the lunar calendar. On that night, as there was no bridge that the Cowherd could use to cross the river, a large group of magpies came to make a bridge, which was called Magpie Bridge. There are two smaller stars beside Altair, and these are the sons.

CHAPTER 8. THE PEONY ARBOR

In the period of the Southern Song Dynasty (1127–1279) there lived a man called Du Bao, the magistrate of NanAn city. He had a daughter, Du LiNiang, who was sixteen now. The magistrate asked an elderly tutor named Chen Zuiliang to teach his daughter at home so the daughter could read and write.

One fine spring day, her handmaid Spring Scent suggested that Miss should have a walk in the back garden as the weather was so nice. The girl thought it a good suggestion and took her maid out to the back garden. They strolled among the trees and flowers. The scene was so colorful and the air so perfumed. They came to an arbor, the Peony Arbor, beside which grew a plum tree.

In Chinese love stories, generally a girl is seen aspiring for a certain boy, especially in spring time. While young Miss Du was strolling in the garden, the thought came to her that as pleasant as this was, how much more pleasant it would be if only she could be here with a boy. But she did not know any boys.

That night, she had a dream. In the dream, she saw a handsome youth coming along the walk with a willow twig in his hand. He asked her to write a poem for him. Then she felt that the boy carried her to the Peony Arbor in the garden and caressed her there.

The next day when she woke up, she did not feel anything

wrong. She went to the garden to seek for any trace of the dream, but found nothing unusual there. She was disappointed and fell lovesick. (That was the general plot of a Chinese love tale.) She ate less and less; she grew leaner and leaner day by day. One day she looked at herself in the mirror and found herself terribly thin. She thought that she might die soon. She got a scroll of white silk and painted her own image on it and wrote a poem on it, too. (Traditionally, a Chinese painter would often create a poem together with a painting.) When the parents were told that their daughter was seriously ill, they asked a doctor to come to look at her and give her medicine, but it was to no avail. Then her parents asked a Taoist nun to come to pray for her.

The girl died of lovesickness on the day of the Mid-Autumn Festival. That was the fifteenth day of the eighth moon in the lunar calendar, an important day. On that day, families have a happy reunion of all their members. Before she died Miss Du told her maid to put her painting in a box of rosewood and hide it under the stone by the small pond in the back garden beside the arbor and the plum tree. Then she asked her parents by bury her coffin under the plum tree, which was accordingly done by her last wish. Moreover, the parents had a kind of temple built in their daughter's memory. The temple was called Plum Temple. They asked the Taoist nun to live in the temple to always pray for their daughter.

At the time, a rebel army under the leadership of Li Quan came to attack Yangzhou city. The emperor ordered Du Bao to go to Yangzhou city to conquer the rebel army. So Du took his wife, Lady Du, and the handmaid, Spring Scent, to the city. When they reached HuaiAn town, Du let his wife and the maid go onward to LinAn city, the capital, so that they could be safe from the dangers of war. Lady Du and the maid went ahead then, and they lived in the capital, waiting for the return of Du Bao.

There was a young man named Liu Mengmei who lived in Canton, Guangdong province. He left home for the capital with the intention of trying his luck at the government examinations. One night he dreamed that he was in a garden and saw a lovely young lady standing under a plum tree, saying to him that she was destined to be his wife. He dismissed the image as a dream. Nothing but a dream.

On his way to the capital, he was suddenly taken ill and had to stop and lodge in a temple. When he was recovered, he went to the back garden to have a walk in the sunshine. He sat on the stone by the small pond and by chance found the box of rose-wood. He took it to his room and opened it. Inside it, he found a picture of a beautiful girl. He seemed to recognize her. Then he remembered that he had seen her in his dream at home. He hung the picture up on the wall in his room and prayed for her every day.

The ghost of Du LiNiang was now in the other world. She had stayed there three years. The king of the other world decided that Du LiNiang should not die so young, and according to her fate she had more tasks ahead of her to be accomplished. Therefore, the king let her go back to the human world.

Now her ghost came to the Plum Temple and saw the young man was praying for her. She was deeply moved and made her appearance as a human, telling him that she was a girl from the neighborhood. They chatted joyfully and fell in love with each other.

A ghost can only move around in the night, in the dark. So the girl came to talk to the young man every evening night and left before dawn. The Taoist nun heard started hearing sounds every night in the young man's room. She was so curious that one night she slipped into the room where he was lodging. When she saw a girl there, she demanded to know the truth. The girl had to tell the young man that she was a ghost, and she asked him to dig up her coffin and open it the next day. So he did, with the help of the Taoist nun. Once the coffin was opened, the ghost of Du LiNiang threw herself into the body, which opened her eyes and got to her feet. The girl was thus revived. Then the trio, the girl and the young man and the Taoist nun, traveled in a boat to LinAn, the capital.

Chen Zuiliang, who had been the tutor of the young lady, would sometimes come to check his former pupil's tomb to see that everything was okay. One day, he visited again and found the tomb had been dug up and the body was gone, nowhere to be found. He thought that the body must have been stolen. But who would steal a body?

He left home and headed for where Du Bao had camped with

his troops. He wanted to tell the father that his daughter's body was missing. On his way there, he was captured by the rebel army. When the leader Li Quan found out that he was the former tutor in Du's family and was now going to see Du, he lied to him that he had killed Lady Du and her maid. He then let Chen go, knowing he would report this to Du.

When Du got the message, he bitterly mourned for his wife and the maid. But he still had to deal with the rebel army. So he wrote a letter to Li Quan and sent Chen to deliver the letter to him. In the letter he promised that if Li would surrender to the government, he would beg the Emperor to forgive him and make him an officer of the government. Li found that a good deal and he accepted. The rebellion was thus resolved.

The young man and the girl and the Taoist nun arrived in LinAn city (the present Hangzhou city), and lodged in an inn. The young man went to participate in the tests and soon he finished them. As far as the Taoist nun knew, the girl's parents had gone to Yangzhou city. While they all were waiting for the results of the tests, the girl asked the young man, now her husband, to go to Yangzhou city to find her parents and tell them about her revival and let them know that she was staying now in LinAn city. So the young man started off for Yangzhou city.

Just at the same time, Du Bao sent his lady and the maid to come to LinAn city. Coincidently, they lodged in the same inn. And they soon found each other. The mother was ecstatic over the revival of her daughter. They joyfully waited together for the arrival of their husband and father as well.

The young man went to find the girl's father and introduced himself as his son-in-law. The father thought that his daughter was already dead, and so it simply could not be that he had a son-in-law. He thought that the young man was a trickster and a liar, so he detained him in the prison. Then, when he returned to the capital to report to the Emperor, he brought the young man under custody to be questioned.

When the father reached the capital, he met his family. As the leader of the rebel army had told him that he had killed his wife and the maid, the father thought they were all ghosts. But the Taoist nun was a living person and she verified the fact that the three persons were all alive. The wife and the maid had never died and the daughter was revived.

In the meantime, the young man came out first in the government examinations, and the Emperor demanded to see him and assigned him an official position. When the father learned the truth, he was overwhelmed with joy. So they had a blessed reunion and lived together pleasantly.

CHAPTER 9. QUEEN DOWAGER XUAN

Let's go back further in the early history of China, to the reign of the Zhou Dynasty (1121 BC–255 BC). The Zhou Dynasty can be divided into two periods: the Western Zhou (1121 BC–771 BC) and the Eastern Zhou (770 BC–255 BC). The Zhou Dynasty overthrew the Shang Dynasty (1765 BC–1121 BC).

The last king of the Shang Dynasty was King Jiu, a tyrant. He killed several wise and faithful courtiers who had advised him to be kind to people and not to live so extravagantly.

King Jiu had a magnificent building constructed, and it was called the Deer Terrace. Almost day and night, he sat there and drank, and watched dancing girls, neglecting his duties. He also had a pond filled with wine and a forest with pieces of cooked meat hung on the branches, where he would take his queen and concubines to have a happy time together.

This extravagance and misconduct drove some courtiers and many people to escape to the Zhou state, which was then only an earldom. The Earl of Zhou was a good-hearted man and treated his courtiers and people well. The earldom turned stronger and stronger, both financially and militarily. At last under the support of other states who could no more endure the tyranny of King Jiu, the Earl of Zhou gathered a large army and marched on the capital of the Shang Dynasty and conquered it. Then the Earl of Zhou set up his Zhou Dynasty and declared himself king.

King Jiu burned himself to death on the Deer Terrace, and that was the end of the Shang Dynasty.

During every dynasty in China, the first few kings tended to be more benevolent and then their successors would become more and more self indulgent, more lax in their administration, till the dynasty collapsed and a new dynasty was born. There was a king of Western Zhou named King Li (on the throne 878 BC–841 BC), who always accused those courtiers whom he disliked of criticizing him in their minds, even though they did not express it openly yet. Historians may ask, if the criticisms were not spoken, how could the king know that some courtiers were criticizing him? But that is what history tells us.

King Li had a very beautiful queen, but she never even smiled, let alone laugh. King Li would think of every way to please his queen to make her smile, but all his efforts were in vain. One evening, he took his queen to the top of Mt. Li near the capital. The spot could command a vast view over the expanse of his territory. There was a watch-tower on the mountain. If any invaders came, the watchman would burn dried wolf-dung, which he collected constantly. The smoke from wolf dung was thick and could not be blown away easily. So when the smoke rose high, it could be seen from afar. Then lords in the neighborhood would come to the rescue with their troops.

One day on the top of Mt. Li, a wonderful idea struck King Li. He ordered the watchman to send up the smoke. Accordingly, the lords rushed to their aid, thinking there were invaders from the north as there lived some different ethnic groups there, who often trespassed into the territory of West Zhou. But when they reached the mountain, with drums beating and banners flying, there were no enemies anywhere to be seen, only the king and his queen sitting on the mountain top. The king sent one of his bodyguards to tell the lords that he was doing this only to entertain his queen. The lords looked at each other in frustration and left, with drums muffled and banners rolled up. Needless to say, a day came when the king and his queen were enjoying the pretty scene, and foreign troops did invade. Though the watchman sent up the smoke signal, none of the vassal lords responded.

The Western Zhou ended when the grandson of King Li, called King You (795 BC–771 BC), was ruling. In 771 BC, a neighboring tribe came to take the capital and killed King You. When his son King Ping (780 BC–720 BC) succeeded the throne, the historians deemed this the beginning of the Eastern Zhou Dynasty, because King Ping relocated his capital to Luoyi in 770 BC, east of the old capital. The capital was relocated because the old capital was destroyed by the invaders they took it.

During the Zhou Dynasty, there were many fiefs such as dukedoms, marquisates, and earldoms. In the Eastern Zhou period, the king gradually became weaker and some dukes, marquises, or counts gradually became strong. A warring period ensued, between 472 BC and 221 BC, during which battle after battle broke out among rival states.

The strong states swallowed up the weaker states and became larger and stronger, till there were only seven states left. They were the Qin state in the west, the Chu state in the south, the Qi state in the east, the Yan state in northeast, and the Han state, Zhao state and Wei state in the north; seven in all. The head of every state declared himself king. They no longer obeyed the king of East Zhou. In 256 BC, East Zhou was merged into the Qin Dynasty. And there, our story takes place.

Queen Dowager Xuan (d. 265 BC), née Mi, was born in the Chu Kingdom. Its territory was connected to the Qin kingdom in the west. In the empire of China, there was a queen, and every concubine of the king or emperor had a palace title. In every dynasty, the title was different. Such titles indicated different ranks. In the Qin Dynasty in that period, the lowest title for a concubine was Bazi. In this case, as Bazi was later married to King Weiwen of the Qin kingdom, she was generally called Mi Bazi in history, and so I will call her in this story.

Mi Bazi was born a princess of the Chu kingdom. But her mother had not received any palace title. While she was a little girl, she showed herself to be lively and beautiful, and a quick learner, so her father, King Wei (d. 329 BC), liked her very much. Her father enjoyed playing with her, which was not considered suitable according to tradition. However, the king ignored that tradition. Only he died early, and Mi Bazi's stepbrother succeeded the throne as King Huai (374 BC–296 BC). His mother became the Queen dowager, and she had always hated the mother of Mi Bazi out of envy and jealousy. Now, as her husband had died, the mother of Mi Bazi lost protection. As she had no palace title, the Queen dowager expelled her and the little girl out of the palace. Thus the rest of Mi Bazi's childhood was spent in poverty and hardship.

Then her mother was married to a commoner and gave birth to a son, so now Mi Bazi had a stepbrother by the name of Wei Ran. (Although he was not of blue blood, since his father was nobody, when he went later to the Qin kingdom, he became a powerful general with the help of his stepsister, Mi Bazi, who married had King Hui of the Qin kingdom.)

After several years, her stepfather died and then her mother died, too. Now only she and her stepbrother survived. She was now a teenager and her stepbrother was just a boy, a few years younger than she. Where could she go now and what would they live on? How could she feed her little stepbrother? She had lived outside the palace with her poor mother for so long, she almost forgot that she was a princess. But now the only way for her was to go back to the palace, and so there she went with her stepbrother.

When she reached the palace gate, she told the guards who she was and asked them to report her visit to her other stepbrother, the king. Although the guards knew that there had once been a young princess who had been driven out of the palace by the Queen dowager, they could not recognize her, as she had grown up, and they were reluctant to make fools of themselves as anyone could come along as an imposter. Nonetheless, one of the guards went in to report to the king that there was a young girl at the gate, making such a claim. The king summoned the princess into his presence. Mi Bazi went in alone, leaving her stepbrother Wei Ran with the guards at the gate.

When the king saw the princess, he looked and looked: and he recognized the expressions and features of her face, though her stature had grown. When they were little, they had often played together. Then the king sent her to see the Queen dowager, who would have to arrange where the princess would live. The Queen Dowager still hated her mother, and of course she also hated the princess. But as the king had permitted her to come back, the Queen dowager could not drive her away again. Therefore, the Queen dowager allocated her a place to live, outside the palace, in a shabby house with modest provisions and necessary clothes, and a small living allowance as palace rules allowed. So she lived there with her stepbrother Wei Ran. From time to time, she went into the palace to see the Queen dowager, her stepmother, and the king, for the sake of etiquette. But she had also the advantage that, living outside the palace, she could act freely and do whatever she liked, with no need to ask permission from the Queen dowager. She came to know a young man by the name of Huang Xie, who was an official with a promising career at the king's court. He was a kind man and often looked after the princess and her stepbrother. The stepbrother learned from Huang Xie how to read and write, and also how to fight as a warrior.

The Queen Dowager had a daughter of her own flesh and blood, Princess Shu, a couple of years older than Mi Bazi. The Queen Dowager treated her own daughter as nicely as she treated Mi Bazi badly. Mi Bazi had to endure the ill-treatment. How could she escape from it?

As there were seven kingdoms at the time, men of talent who found that their abilities were not appreciated and who were not given suitable positions could go to other kingdoms to try their luck. But Mi Bazi could not escape to other kingdoms to seek a living. She was a princess of the Chu kingdom, and her best be was still to stay there. However, she was even afraid that the Queen dowager would kill her some day.

Mi Bazi goes to the Qin kingdom

In the warring period, every king wanted to subdue the others and unite China under his own leadership. At that time warriors generally fought riding on chariots. But the Zhao kingdom learned something important from the nomads in the north: they abandoned chariots and began to train their soldiers to fight directly on horseback. This made them far more nimble than those riding in chariots and gave them a great advantage. Then the Qin kingdom learned this skill, too. Gradually the Qin kingdom got stronger than the other six kingdoms. The other kingdoms feared that the Qin kingdom would conquer them one by one. There was a strategist named Su Qin (d. 284 BC) who went round to the six kingdoms and persuaded the kings to form an alliance against the Qin kingdom. All the six kings thought that this was a good idea, and so they appointed Su Qin as their minister in charge of the alliance.

Around the same time, another strategist by the name of Zhang Yi (d. 310 BC) went to the Qin kingdom to persuade King Hui that he had a ruse to break up that alliance. If they could estrange the six kings from each other and sow distrust among them, they could be brought to befriend the Qin kingdom. King Hui believed him and made him the prime minister of the Qin kingdom, and also endowed him with six square li of land as his fief.

Then Zhang Yi went to the Chu kingdom to see King Huai of Chu. He said to King Huai that King Hui of Qin would offer him 600 square li of land if the King of Chu allied with him and desert his other allies. Besides, King Hui of Qin would marry a Chu princess so that the two kingdoms would be marital allies forever. The King of Chu was not too smart, but he had some ambition, so he jumped at an offer that sounded so good.

When the Queen dowager learned of this, she decided to marry her own daughter, Princess Shu, to the King of Qin. Of course it was considered a great honor that a princess could marry a king. So preparations were made to send Princess Shu to the Qin kingdom, a great distance away. Careful arrangements were made so that Princess Shu would be presented in the best light, and so she would be sent with many trunks filled with valuables, including jewels and scrolls of silk. She would take some maids to serve her and a brigade of soldiers would escort her to the frontier, where troops of the Qin kingdom would take over her protection and escort her to the capital of Qin.

Mi Bazi still wanted to leave the Chu kingdom for her safety. When she learned the news, she sensed the chance coming. She was clever and knew how to defend her interests. By tradition, the bride had to take along a couple of bridesmaids. Not everyone might be pleased to be sent so far away to an unknown family in an unknown land, but she wanted to be one of the bridesmaids. She made up her mind to go and see the Queen dowager. She offered herself as a bridesmaid, saying that as the stepsister of Princess Shu she could better look after her. The Queen Dowager had always disliked her and now she thought this was a fine chance to get rid of her forever. She agreed to Mi Bazi's suggestion, and both got what they needed.

Mi Bazi took her stepbrother Wei Ran with her to the Qin kingdom. Wei Ran was still under age and she could not leave him behind alone. There were coaches for the ladies to ride in. Mi Bazi rode in the first coach. Princess Shu rode in the second coach and the other bridesmaid in the third coach. Two maids who were to wait on the princess were in the fourth coach. All the men rode on horseback while the common soldiers were on foot. There were also some wagons carrying all the trunks. As the King of Chu saw off the procession as it was leaving the capital, he was glad that he was making a strong marital ally. He sent an envoy along to receive the grant to 600 square li of land when they arrived in the Qin capital.

Kidnapped by the Yiju Tribe

The marriage procession proceeded smoothly within the territory of the Chu kingdom. When they reached the border of the two kingdoms, the Qin troops were waiting there to welcome them. Then the Chu soldiers turned back toward their capital while the Qin troops escorted the coaches and wagons to the Qin capital. King Hui of Qin got the news and had all the preparations made for the reception and wedding ceremony.

Close by the Qin kingdom, there lived a nomadic tribe called the Yiju. They were real fierce fighters on horseback. They often trespassed into Qin territory to rob Qin people and then returned to their own camps with the loot. When the chieftain of the Yiju heard that such a well-endowed marriage procession was coming from the Chu kingdom, he planned to rob them—of course. And if possible, he would take the Chu princess for his own wife.

When the procession turned the corner of at the base of a cliff, the Yiju fighters rushed out from a slope, giving war cries. The procession had to stop and the troops arranged themselves into battle array. When the fight started, the chieftain broke through and rode to the first coach, as he thought that the princess should be in that coach. But it was Mi Bazi whom he captured, and he ran away with his supposed bride.

When the Yiju fighters left, the procession and the troops resumed their way to the capital. The King of Qin received his bride in the palace and in due course they were married in a grand wedding ceremony. Afterwards, it was reported to the king that one bridesmaid had been kidnapped by Yiju fighters. He summoned Zhang Yi, his prime minister, and asked him about the missing bridesmaid. Before coming to the Qin kingdom, Zhang Yi had lived in the Chu kingdom. He had talked to the King of Chu in hopes that the king could give him a suitable position, but the king did not trust him. That was why he had left the Chu kingdom for the Qin kingdom. When he was staying in the Chu kingdom, he had met with Mi Bazi and known the girl to be a beautiful, wise teenager. Therefore, he told the king everything he knew about Mi Bazi. The king wanted to get the girl back and get to know her better. He ordered Zhang Yi to go to the Yiju to negotiate. If the Yiju could release the girl, they would be given food grain and horse fodder for the winter. That was a great incentive for them, and winter was coming soon.

After the royal wedding, the envoy from the Chu kingdom went to see Zhang Yi to demand the 600 li of land. Zhang Yi pretended to be surprised to hear this. He said, "Your king, His Majesty, must have heard wrong. I offered only six li of land; that is my own fief. I have no right to give away such a huge piece of land belonging to the Qin kingdom." By turn, the envoy was stunned. He had to return to the Chu kingdom and report this to the king. King Huai was enraged, but he could do nothing at the moment. He planned to take the land by force some day. For now, the Qin kingdom was stronger than the Chu kingdom. He should wait for the right time to act.

How had the Qin kingdom become stronger than the others? It was because the Qin kingdom had undertaken certain reforms. Before the reforms, all members of the nobility by birth enjoyed every benefit and occupied high positions automatically. After the reforms, only those who showed their merit by fighting on the battlefield could be assigned such high positions and enjoy all the benefits. The nobility were of course opposed to this rule, but the king supported it. And the Qin people approved because it made conditions equal for everyone who could earn such honor through personal endeavor. The nobility no longer had all the advantages just by birth. So several years into its implementation, this new arrangement made the Qin kingdom stronger.

Mi Bazi becomes a concubine of the king

Let's get back to Mi Bazi. The chieftain took her to his tent. Her great beauty made her irresistibly attractive. He talked to Mi Bazi and asked her to be his wife. That was, of course, out of the question. At that time, people living in the six kingdoms were considered civilized while the tribes and nomads were deemed barbarians. A civilized person could never marry a barbarian. Now, barbarian that he was, the chieftain could certainly have raped her, but he found her so extraordinary that he did not wish to force her to be his wife. He wanted her to marry him with her free will. So Mi Bazi lived with the Yiju tribe for a while. Almost all the Yiju men found her attractive, as she was a kind and pleasant person as well as a beauty. She was especially kind to a boy who parents had died when he was still a baby. Now she took care of him and looked upon him as her brother.

It was a couple of months later when Zhang Yi made it to the Yiju camps. Mi Bazi was delighted to see Zhang Yi again in such an awkward situation. The deal was done as the Yiju really needed the grain and fodder for the coming winter, and Zhang Yi took Mi Bazi to the King of Qin. The King liked her immediately and recognized her wisdom as well as her great beauty. He therefore made her his royal concubine and gave her the palace title of Bazi. Hence, she was known in the history by this title plus her family name Mi.

To test her wisdom, the king often discussed state affairs with her and asked her opinion about certain events. What she said was always right to the point. Therefore, by degrees, she became the king's favorite woman, not by her beauty, but by her wisdom.

How did the king spend his days? Let's take a look. He would have the levée in the morning, discussing state affairs with courtiers and making decisions on the spot. When the situation was stable, the courtiers were then dismissed and the king retired to his study to read reports that courtiers had handed in from the previous days. After reading every report, the king wrote on it his opinion or decision. Then he gave the report with his opinion on it back to the courtier who had written it, or gave the report with his decision on it to the concerned department to be carried out. Sometimes if the king did not feel well, he would let Mi Bazi read the reports for him and then instructed her as to what to write on them. Thus, Mi Bazi learned how to handle state affairs. The experience helped her later, as she eventually held the regency as her son was still under age when he succeeded the throne. She was the first Queen Dowager with political power in the history of China.

Fighting to be crown prince

King Hui of Qin loved Mi Bazi, but his queen was the former Princess Shu, Mi Bazi's stepsister. She was soon pregnant and she bore a son for the king. The son was named Ying (family name) Dang, Prince Dang (325 BC–307 BC). The king had already several sons and daughters born by his concubines. According to feudal tradition, the son of the queen was generally made crown prince, and he would duly succeed his father to the throne. But the present king still had the right to assign the position of crown prince to his eldest son or one of the other sons, for instance one born of his favorite concubine.

In the same year when the Queen gave birth to her son Ying Dang, Mi Bazi also bore the king a son. He was named Ying Ji, Prince Ji (325 BC–251 BC). The son of the Queen grew stout and strong, and liked to show his strength by lifting heavy weights, while the son of the favorite concubine was of normal size and preferred to immerse himself in the study of all sorts of books. The Queen's son was impulsive, acting before thinking things through, while the son of the favorite concubine acted only after deep consideration. Everyone could see that the King preferred the son of the favorite concubine to be his successor. Therefore, the Queen began to bribe important courtiers to support her son as the crown prince. Mi Bazi did not want to vie with the Queen, her stepsister, and argue over whose son should be the crown prince. But the Queen could not conceive of that—she could only imagine that everyone else would do the same as she was doing, and so she assumed that her stepsister would vie with her to make her son the crown prince. Thus, the Queen began to hate her stepsister for no reason. And a few times, the Queen schemed with her supporters to do harm to the son of her stepsister, but it was all in vain.

The Qin kingdom conquered region of Bashu

Mi Bazi was a true strategist. She let her younger stepbrother Wei Ran join the army under General Sima Cuo so that Wei Ran could have an opportunity to rise in social status or even to become a general. At that time, the Qin kingdom wished to expand its territory.

Once during a levée, a question was raised as to where the Qin army should attack first. Zhang Yi suggested that the Qin must assault the Han kingdom first so that they could march further east to conquer others. General Sima Cuo opposed the idea and argued that such an undertaking was too big at present for the Qin to realize. The best way, he suggested, was to take over the region of Bashu (the present Sichuan province) in the west, as there were riots there and it would be easy to win the battle—and easy to win over the people afterward. Once they occupied the region, they could have grain growing there for the army and also enroll the people into the army.

Besides, if they attacked the Han kingdom first, other kingdoms would protest or even unite against the Qin kingdom. If the Qin took over Bashu, none of other kingdom would say anything against it. The only difficulty was that the way to Bashu was blocked by rugged mountains and cliffs. But Sima Cuo said, "I have a stratagem to overcome the difficulty." So the king let him take the full charge to conquer Bashu by whatever means he thought fit.

Sima chose a route what was comparatively smooth and he ordered that some cows crafted of gold should be planted there. When the people of Bashu saw them, they would dig a way through the mountains themselves just to get the golden cows back to Bashu. So it happened, just as Sima planned. Then Sima led his army into Bashu and occupied it in 316 BC.

During the fighting, Wei Ran showed his mettle and won merit, starting gradually and finally being promoted to general. Then Mi Bazi beseeched the king to give the region as the fief of her son, Prince Ji. The king promised to do so, but he had no time to issue his edict yet.

How the Queen's son became the crown prince

The health of King Hui was declining, and the courtiers implored him to name the son of the Queen as crown prince. Under such pressure and also considering his poor health, the king had to make the son the crown prince, his successor. One day in 311 BC, King Hui died and the crown prince became King Wu, or King Wuli. Although the matter of the succession was settled, the Queen still wished her stepsister to suffer and so she told her son, now king, to send his brother, Prince Ji, son of Mi Bazi, to the Yan kingdom as a hostage for the purpose of sealing an alliance to deal with the Qi kingdom. (The late king had a daughter who had been married off to the King of Yan. She was a stepsister of Prince Ji.) Then his mother, Mi Bazi, would follow him to the Yan kingdom.

The young King Wu was fond of fighting and in 308 BC, he gave orders to attack Yiyang town of the Han kingdom. Next year the Qin kingdom took the town, and the Han kingdom lost 600,000 soldiers killed by the Qin army. The Han kingdom had to seek a truce with the Qin kingdom.

King Wu went there for the negotiations, and by way of the Han kingdom, he went to Luoyang city, the capital of the Eastern Zhou to look at the famous nine giant bronze three-legged urns, symbolic of the urns that were used as cooking pots or decoration in ancient China. History recorded that when the King of Zhou subdued the Shang Dynasty, there were nine regions in China. The King of Zhou demanded that every region should give him some hundred catties of bronze. He used the bronze from the nine regions to be cast into nine urns, one for each region with the name of the region engraved on it. So the urns became the symbol of reign. King Wu went there to look at the urns, which implied that he intended to unite China and to be king of kings.

There was a famous warlord called Meng Fen there. King Wu, with all his braggadocio, wanted to compete with him by lifting an urn to see who was stronger. But in the process, he broke his leg and died in the city in the eighth moon of that year. He was on the throne only for four years.

As King Wu had produced no son in that short time, all the sons of King Hui started to fight each other for the throne. None of the sons was strong enough to conquer the others, and the kingdom fell into chaos. Then General Wei Ran, the stepbrother of Mi Bazi, together with other courtiers and helped by King Wuling of the Zhao kingdom, got Prince Ji and his mother Mi Bazi back to the Qin kingdom. They supported this son to be the next king of the Qin kingdom.

He became King Zhaoxiang, or simply King Zhao. He was the king who sat the longest on the throne out of all the kings of the Qin Dynasty. Since at this time King Zhao was still under age, his mother held the regency. She was offered the title of Queen Dowager. She was the first, and the last, Queen Dowager in the history of China. That was because the Qin kingdom would soon be turned into an empire, after the Qin kingdom united all of China. Thereafter, in subsequent dynasties, there were emperors and empresses, and any dowager would be Empress Dowager, not Queen Dowager.

How Mi Bazi restored the peace

When King Zhao first took the throne, there was still the chaos in the kingdom. The queen, Mi Bazi's stepsister, was afraid that now Queen Dowager Bazi would kill her, and so she escaped to Prince Hua, the stepbrother of King Hui, whose fief was in the northern part of the kingdom and who was one of those vying for the throne. He was a better fighter than the other sons. Queen Dowager Shu promised to support him to be the king if he could defeat Queen Dowager Bazi.

Now Queen Dowager Bazi had to seek more support to win the war. The other sons, under the instigation of Queen Shu, united to fight Queen Dowager Bazi.

Bazi could not easily defeat the allied army. She thought of the chieftain of the Yiju tribe, who could be a possible ally to help her. Therefore, she dispatched a messenger to summon the chieftain to the capital of the Qin kingdom. The chieftain was pleased that he could see the woman he loved again. He brought all his fighters and helped Queen Dowager Bazi to defeat the united army of the sons. The young boy whom Bazi had cared for while she was staying with the Yiju was now a strong man and could fight bravely. He also won merit during the wars and gradually he was promoted to be a general, too, by Queen Dowager Bazi. This meant that he was now a general of the Qin kingdom, no longer a Yiju fighter. All the sons surrendered and were exiled to their own fiefs. Only Prince Hua died in a battle. Queen Shu was captured and taken to the capital. She feared that her stepsister would kill her, but Queen Dowager Bazi only confined her to the rooms where she had always lived. She would live there until death.

The chieftain looked upon himself as a savior to Queen Dowager Bazi, and he went to live in the palace with her as husband and wife. Afterwards, Bazi did marry him and even bore two sons with him. One boy became a general of the Qin kingdom and was named Bai Qi (d. 257 BC). He was nicknamed "the god of killing," because he killed so many soldiers of other kingdoms in battles. He slew 340,000 soldiers of the united army of the Han and Wei kingdoms. And a few years later, he killed 130,000 soldiers of the Wei kingdom and buried alive 400,000 surrendered soldiers of the Zhao kingdom.

This was a famous war in the early history of China. It happened at Changping town, and so it was called War of Changping. The commander of the army of the Zhao kingdom was Zhao Gua, who often boasted that he had read many books about strategies of war that his late father had left for him. But the strategy Bai Qi adopted was better than that of Zhao Gua. The army of the Zhao kingdom was defeated and Zhao Gua was killed. So historians laughed at Zhao Gua, saying that he read his father's books for nothing.

The Yiju fighters, though they remained camped outside the city, often came into the city for supplies or to get a taste of town life. But they did not know the traditions of the civil people of the Qin kingdom. They often offended shop owners and waiters, or even the common people in the streets, when the fighters walked to and fro, staring with curiosity at almost everything in the city. So people of the Qin kingdom often complained about the misbehavior of the Yiju fighters. When Queen Dowager Bazi learned what people of the Qin kingdom thought of the Yiju men, she told the chieftain to restrain his men, but the chieftain did not agree to do so. He thought that his men should be free to do whatever they liked. So Queen Dowager Bazi and the chieftain had a quarrel. As the situation grew worse, Queen Dowager Bazi forbade the Yiju fighters to come into the city. But the chieftain and his men refused to obey. Then the people in the city grew angrier and angrier, till one day for the safety and goodness of her own people, Queen Dowager Bazi had to have the chieftain killed. The Yiju tribe was conquered and their land was merged into the Qin kingdom.

Now the son of Queen Dowager Bazi, the present king of the Qin kingdom, came of age and could handle state affairs, albeit still with the help of his mother. Sometimes he would make decisions independently.

How King Huai of Chu died in the Qin kingdom

King Huai of Chu was so changeable in attitude towards other kingdoms. Sometimes he united with the Han, Zhao and Wei kingdoms in the north, and then he sided with the Qin kingdom. So the three kingdoms of Han, Zhao and Wei allied against the Chu kingdom. Now the King of Chu was afraid that the three kingdoms in the north would invade his kingdom together. Therefore, he sent his crown prince to the Qin kingdom as a hostage in return for the support of the Qin kingdom. That was how things were done at that time between kingdoms, something like assigning your collateral in order to secure a loan.

After a year, the Crown Prince of Chu had a dispute with an official of Qin and they began to fight. The Crown Prince hit the official and accidentally killed him. He was afraid that the King of Qin would kill him for that, so he escaped back to Chu. The King of the Qin kingdom was indeed infuriated and he allied with the Qi kingdom to attack the Chu kingdom. The King of Chu sent his crown prince to the Qi kingdom as a hostage and the Qi kingdom broke its alliance with the Qin kingdom.

Then the King of Qin wrote to the King of Chu, asking him to come to the Qin kingdom to talk the matter over. Some of the Chu courtiers advised the king not to go, fearful that the Qin kingdom would hold him captive. However, another son of King Huai, called Zilan, urged his father to go lest the Qin kingdom invade them for sure. The king hesitated because of the great risk. At length, the king decided that he had better go to the Qin kingdom in hopes of placating them, and perhaps he could forestall their invasion.

Anyway, as soon as the King of Chu crossed the border into the Qin kingdom, he was detained and taken to the capital. The King of Qin never summoned him to the palace, as if he was a courtier of Qin, not the King of Chu. The King of Qin proposed that if King Huai wished to return to his kingdom, he must grant a large piece of land to the Qin kingdom. That was the condition. But King Huai rejected it. So he remained confined, and in the end King Huai died in the Qin kingdom. Back in the Chu kingdom, where the crown prince was a hostage in the Qi kingdom, the son Zilan made himself King of Chu. In 265 BC, Queen Dowager Bazi died and was buried at Mt. Li in the area of the present XiAn city.

CHAPTER 10. THE TALE OF PAN JINLIAN AND THE DWARF

This story took place in the Northern Song Dynasty (960 BC–AD 1127). There lived a beautiful girl, about twenty years old, in Qinghe town. She was only a maid working for a rich family. The master of the family, though quite old, still enjoyed young girls. He wanted to take Pan Jinlian for his concubine, but she was not willing to marry an old man. She went to tell the mistress, the wife of the master, an old lady, about this. The wife was so jealous that she married off the maid to an ugly dwarf in Wujia village, close to the city. Although Pan Jinlian was loath to marry the dwarf, she could not defy the old lady.

Almost all the families in Wujia village had the surname of Wu. The dwarf had the name of Wu Dalang, and he had a younger brother called Wu Song. Wu song was tall and handsome, and was skilled in kungfu. Villagers wondered how a dwarf could have such a brother from the same mother. Their parents had died long ago, and the brothers had a big difference of age. So when their parents died, the dwarf, being much older, took care of the younger brother Wu Song and brought him up to manhood. Wu Song traveled all over the province and made his living by doing odd jobs.

Wu Dalang lived from hand to mouth, making and sell pancakes. He got up early to make pancakes, then he went out carrying a basketful of pancakes for sale. In the evening when he had sold all the pancakes, he went home to rest. He ate pancakes himself, three meals a day. A poor orphan boy called YunGe lived as a beggar, and Wu Dalang looked after him by sometimes giving the boy a pancake or two.

Pan Jinlian now lived with Wu Dalang and cooked breakfast and supper for him every day. Wu Dalang just ate his own pancakes for lunch. Although Pan Jinlian was dissatisfied with her life with the dwarf, they lived peacefully like a dear husband and wife, and they went like this for a few years.

Wu Song, brother of the dwarf, got tired of the vagabond life, and now he repaired to his home town to re-unite with his brother. He thought he would like to live with his brother, his sole flesh and blood, for the rest of his life, and when his brother grew old, he would take care of him.

One evening on his way back home, he saw a tavern at a distance and wanted to have something to fill his stomach. As he approached, he saw a public notice on the outside wall of the tavern. It warned that recently a tiger had appeared from nowhere. The local yamen warned travelers not to go over the mountain alone. They should form groups or take a detour for their own safety.

Wu Song ignored the warning, however, thinking that with his kungfu, he had no need to fear a tiger. Thus, after eating something, he went on his way to the mountain. Half way over the steep climb, he did hear a wild roar. Then he saw a tiger coming out from behind a rock. As the tiger saw a man, a good meal, it first crouched, then with an echoing roar, he jumped forth toward Wu Song. Wu Song leaped aside and the tiger passed him. When the tiger landed on the ground on its four paws, Wu Song jumped up and landed on the tiger's back, astride. He put his left hand on the neck of the tiger to push its head on the ground and he formed his right hand into a fist. He hit the head of the tiger continuously till the tiger stirred no more. He got up and kicked the tiger on the side to make sure it was dead. Then he continued his way. At the foot of the mountain, he met some hunters, who had come, by the order of the mayor, to kill the tiger. Wu Song told them that he had already killed the tiger and that they could take it to the mayor.

Wu Song was thus deemed a hero by the townspeople. The mayor sent for him to the yamen and asked him to be the head of the yamen's police force. Wu Song was glad to accept the position since he had to have a job to earn a living. The townspeople carried him on a sedan in a parade round the town. Then Wu Song was allowed to go to see his brother.

Wu Dalang was at home at that very time, talking to Pan Jinliang about his heroic brother. Right at that moment, Wu Song came in, and Wu Dalang introduced him to Pan Jinlian, now his sister-in-law, who had prepared some food for supper to celebrate the return and the heroic deed of Wu Song.

Wu Song had a few days off before he went on duty at the yamen. He stayed at home while his brother went out to sell pancakes. Wu Song was so manly, compared with his dwarf brother. Pan Jinlian found him very attractive and she wished she could seduce him so that she would know what real love was like. Therefore, she prepared some tasty food and wine, and asked her brother-in-law to sit down at the table for lunch. After eating and drinking, she hinted to Wu Song, but he refused. This happened several times while Wu Dalang was out selling pancakes, till one day Wu Song could stand it no longer. A loyal brother, he moved to the lodge at the yamen.

Pan Jinlian and Ximen Qing

In Qinghe town, Ximen Qing was the son of another wealthy family who owned several drug stores. Ximen Qing had a weakness for beautiful women and had a few concubines besides his wife. He had a wide network of connections with powerful men, including the mayor of the town.

One day in the afternoon, Pan Jinlian stood at the window in the second-floor room, looking at the crowds in the street below. Coincidentally, Ximen Qing was in the crowd in that street. Suddenly, the handkerchief that Pan Jinlian was holding fell from her hand accidentally on the head of Ximen Qing, who looked up and was stunned at witnessing such a beauty as he had never seen in his life. Presently, Pan Jinlian opened the door and stepped out. She took the handkerchief Simen Qing handed to her. After Pan Jinlian was back in the house and shut the door,

Ximen Qing knocked at the next door, where an old woman lived, a matchmaker called Old Wang. Old Wang opened the door and recognized Ximen Qing. She smiled broadly and welcomed him into her house. Some of his concubines had been introduced to him by this woman.

When Old Wang asked why Ximen Qing was dropping in at this moment, Ximen Qing told her that he liked the beautiful woman next door. He wished that Old Wang could come up with some means to satisfy his desire. Old Wang told him that she would ask Pan Jinlian (now Ximen Qing learned the name of the beauty) to come over the next day to sew some clothes for her. Old Wang knew that Pan Jinlian was good at sewing. She wanted Ximen Qing to come a bit earlier and hide in the next room. She would give him a signal to emerge from the hiding place. So the plan was perfect.

Next day when Wu Dalang left home to sell pancakes after breakfast, Pan Jinlian went next door. Old Wang took her to her bedroom and produced some pieces of cloth for her to cut and sew. Old Wang told her that she had something to do downstairs. That was the signal for Ximen Qing to come out from his hiding place. So when the old woman went downstairs, Ximen Qing came into the bedroom where Pan Jinlian sat working on the cloth. As Ximen Qing entered, Pan Jinlian looked up and recognized him as the man who returned her handkerchief. Ximen Qing was also a tall and handsome man, the type she liked. When she had first set sight on him, her heart leaped wildly. Today they met again. They did not need any urging from anyone else. From then on, they met each other every few days.

How Wu Dalang died

One day the poor boy YunGe saw Ximen Qing leaving the house of Old Wang and a few minutes later, Pan Jinlian came out and entered her own house. His curiosity was roused, and so he sat by the door of a store across the street from the house of Old Wang and watched Ximen Qing and Pan Jinlian came out one after another at regular intervals. He suspected that something was going on. So he went out to find Wu Dalang as he was on his way home and told him his suspicion. They agreed that whenever YunGe saw Ximen Qing came to visit Old Wang, he would immediately run to fetch Wu Dalang so that he could get into the house and catch them.

One day YunGe did run up to him and they both hurried to Old Wang's house. Wu Dalang left his basket in the hands of YunGe and he himself approached to knock on the door. When Old Wang opened the door, she was astonished to see Pan Jinlian'a husband. Wu Dalang pushed the door wide open and shoved Old Wang aside. He rushed upstairs as best he could and entered the bedroom. It happened so suddenly that Pan Jinlian could only shiver on the bed while Ximen Qing jumped up and kicked Wu Dalang in the stomach. Wu Dalang fell down and spat blood. Ximen Qing, being trained in kungfu, had hit heavily. Ximen Qing got dressed in a hurry and fled while Pan Jinlian quickly put on her clothes and tried to help Wu Dalang to his feet. They both went home and Wu Dalang lay in bed. He was badly injured. At this time, his brother Wu Song was away from town on a●n errand.

Now Wu Dalang was sick in bed and took herbs boiled in water as prescribed by a doctor every day, but he did not feel any better. Pan Jinlian fell into a great fright. If Wu Song learned about the accident, she was in danger and even could lose her life. So she and Ximan Qing met once more at Old Wang's to discuss what to do about this accident. Ximen Qing gave her a small packet of arsenic and instructed her to put it in the bowl of the boiled herbs. Accordingly, Wu Dalang died.

Pan Jinlian reported her husband's death to the yamen, which by law sent a coroner to the house. The coroner concluded that the victim had died of arsenic poisoning. But Ximen bribed the coroner, who changed his conclusion to death by natural causes, that is, disease. The coroner was afraid of Ximen Qing who was a good friend of the mayor. When the coroner was ordered to burn the corpse, he took home a leg bone from the ashes. The bone was black, which was a sign that the person had died of poisoning. He hid the bone and the bribe money in a safe place.

Wu Song's revenge for his brother

After a long while, Wu Song returned from his business tour. The yamen gave him a few days' vacation. He went to visit his brother, whom he had not seen in a long time. As soon as he entered the house, he was surprised to see a memorial tablet with his brother's name written on it on a long table against the wall opposite the door. His sister-in-law was kneeling before the memorial tablet all in white, the color of mourning dress in ancient China. So his brother was already dead. When he asked his sister-in-law how his brother had died, she answered that according to the coroner he had contracted a disease. Wu Song did not say anything more and left. On his way to the yamen, YunGe came up to him and told him what he knew. Therefore, Wu Song went to see the coroner, who told him the truth and produced a black leg bone and bribery money as evidence.

Next day, Wu Song went to his brother's house and invited some neighbors to come over. Old Wang was among the neighbors. He told the neighbors the truth of his brother's death and showed the evidence. He asked the neighbors to be witnesses. He drew out a knife and cut off the heads of Pan Jinlian and Old Wang. He took the two heads to the yamen, followed by the neighbors. The mayor heard the story, but decided that Wu Song had committed the crime of murder—though he had the right reason to do so. Thus, he was sentenced to exile for life.

After a few days, two yamen policemen were to escort Wu Song as a prisoner to the destination he was sentenced for. Before they started down the road, the wicked Ximen Qing bribed the two yamen policemen to kill Wu Song on the way there. A couple of days later, they came to a forest. It was a bit hot in the early afternoon, and the two yamen policemen announced that they wanted to take a nap, but they were afraid that Wu Song would take the chance to escape. Wu Song swore that he would not run away while they had a nap. They could do that without worry. But the two men said that they did not trust him. They wanted to bind Wu Song to a tree trunk while they were napping. So Wu Song let them bind him on a tree trunk. When this was done, the two men drew out their swords, saying that it was Ximen Qing who wanted them to kill him, nothing to do with them. So Wu Song's ghost must take its revenge on Ximen Qing, not on them.

Wu Song used his kungfu to break the rope that tied him to the tree, and he killed the two men with their own swords. Now Wu Song went back to the town and looked for Ximen

Qing. He knew that he would be either in a drinking hall or in a whorehouse.

One day he saw Ximen Qing on his way to his usual haunts, and he pursued him. On the second floor, he saw Ximen Qing sitting at a table by the window. Wu Song dashed forward and pounced. Ximen Qing saw the tiger-killing hero and wanted to escape. He jumped out the window down to the street, but Wu Song followed. They fought in the street. At length Wu Song slew Ximen Qing. This time, Wu Song did not submit himself to the yamen. He just left the town and went to join the rebels in Mt. Liang, in Shandong province. But that's another story.

CHAPTER 11. QIN XIANGLIAN DESERTED BY HER HUSBAND

System of government tests

This story also happened in the Northern Song Dynasty. There lived a well-to-do family in Chenjia village of HeNan province. The surname of most families in that village was Chen. That well-do-do family had a son called Chen Shimei, who was married to a pleasing young woman named Qin Xianglian. They had two children, a boy and a girl. Chen Shimei was a young scholar, that is, a learned man. Every learned man wished to have a bright future by becoming a government official. To be a government official, he must pass three government tests.

The first test was held by the town he lived in. If he passed the first test, he could be admitted to the second test, held by provincial government in the province capital. If he passed the second test, he was entitled to take the third test, held by the central government in the capital. If he could pass the third test, he became a government official and could be assigned a position either in the central government or in a local government, perhaps as mayor of some town.

The ten men who passed with the best grades in the third test would be given an additional test in the palace, right before the Emperor, who would give a theme for the ten winners to write about. Then the Emperor would decide who were the first three winners, and they would be given a feast in the palace, dining with the Emperor. Then they would still have another honor, to ride on horseback for a parade round the capital so that the people could know them. This test was held by the central government every three years. Don't think that only young men were taking the tests. There were, indeed, some old scholars, though very few, who insisted on taking the tests, though they failed every time, yet still held the hope of passing the next, next time, till they grew old.

This system was designed to provide an equal chance for rich and poor scholars, but the rich could bribe the test examiner while the poor could not, and gradually this became common. Although the name of the test-taker was by rule covered so that the test paper examiner could not know which test paper belonging to which test-taker, yet the test-taker could make a little mark or let the bribery-taking examiner know the handwriting of the test-taker beforehand.

This system of using government tests to choose officials began from the Sui Dynasty (581–618) and continued through the Qing Dynasty (1644–1911), and was abolished only with the founding of the first republic–The Republic of China, beginning in 1912.

How Chen Shimei married a princess

Chen Shimei was so ambitious that he wanted to be a government high official, as high as possible—and the highest was the prime minister. He passed the first test when he was eighteen, and then he got married. He passed the second test when he was twenty, and by then he already had his second child. He went to the capital for the third test at the age of twenty-two. He was handsome and looked manly. He arrived in the capital a bit early. As a matter of fact, every test-taker came early. No one wanted to be late to miss the test and live in regret.

Chen Shimei lodged at an inn. He did not have any relative or friend in the capital that he could stay with. Staying at the inn, he had nothing else to do but review the books he had brought with him for the test. At last, the test day came and every test-taker was allowed to enter the test building. Everyone was assigned a small cubicle in which he could write his test paper. There were some test-watchers patrolling in the whole place to see that no one broke the regulations. When anyone finished before the time was up, he could hand in his test paper and then he was permitted to leave. Sometimes, at the end of the time limit, there were still some test-takers who had not yet finished writing, and the test-watcher would come to collect their papers.

Then for a few days, the examiners would read the test papers and decide who had passed and who had failed. When the procedure was over, the names of those who had passed would be written on a paper and posted on the wall of the building, so that every test-taker could come to check if his name was there. Those whose names were on the paper shouted in joy and those who failed left the capital crestfallen like a defeated rooster.

The name of Chen Shimei was among the first few. That meant he could go to the palace for the next test.

The emperor sat on the throne. The ten final test-takers were each given a small table in the space down from the throne where the courtiers generally stood during levées. A joss stick was burned to mark the time. When the joss stick burned up, the test time was finished and the test papers had to be handed in.

When the test-takers were writing, the Emperor sitting above looked round at each of them. The emperor had a daughter, the princess. He intended to select a man to be her husband. When the test time was up, the head eunuch collected the papers and gave them to the Emperor. The test-takers left the palace while the Emperor retired to his study to read the papers. When he finished reading, he decided that Chen Shimei was the first among the ten. He had noticed when he sat on his throne that Chen Shimei was the most suitable man for his daughter. Therefore, by examination and by sight the Emperor made his decision that Chen Shimei should be the husband of his daughter. What the Emperor decided could not be rejected, or the person concerned would be beheaded. In this case, there was an exception: if the man selected was already married, he was allowed not to comply, after he reported the situation to the Emperor.

But Chen Shimei was an ambitious man. He wished to climb to the highest level that could be reached. Such a chance was seldom conferred to an ordinary man like him. So he concealed the fact of his marriage. He even lied that his parents had already died, because if his parents were still living, the Emperor must by tradition give them titles, and even allow them to come to reside in the capital, and then the truth would be revealed. Therefore, he had to lie. But this was cheating, and cheating to the Emperor was also a capital crime. Maybe Chen Shimei forgot that. His wisdom was clouded by his ambition.

At any rate, the imperial wedding took place in due course of time after the necessary preparations. Generally, unmarried princess dwelt in the palace, but once they got married, they would be given residences to live in with their husbands. Now, although the imperial son-in-law had a very high status, he had to salute the princess by kowtowing to her and must obey her, whatever she said. Other than that, all the courtiers had to show him respect. Chen Shimei really enjoyed the life he was leading. He forgot his wife and children at home.

Qin Xianglian comes looking for her husband

It was almost three years since the parents and Qin Xianglian, the wife, had any information from Chen Shimei. No letter came whatsoever. The parents even suspected that their son had died of some accident, or been killed by outlaws on the way to the capital. Then there was a famine and the parents died. Therefore, Qin Xianglian determined to go to the capital on her own to look for her husband. She took the two children with her. They experienced hardship all the way to the capital as they had little money. At last they reached there.

Once she was inside the city, she asked everyone she met if they had heard of Chen Shimei and where she could find him. Now, since Chen Shimei was the imperial son-in-law, almost everyone in the city knew him. She was told where she could find him. So she went there with the children.

When she got to the door of the residence of the princess and asked to see Chen Shimei, the doorman asked who she was. She replied, "I am the wife of Chen Shimei and the children are his son and daughter." The doorman was baffled to think that the bridegroom had a wife and children; if that were so, how could he marry the princess? But it was none of his business. It was up to him whether he let the woman see Chen Shimei, and so he had to drive away the woman and children. Qin Xianglian could not do anything but leave the place. They couldn't lodge at an inn because what little money they had was needed to buy food. Qin Xianglian remembered that she had seen a crumbled joss house outside the city. They had to stay there for the night.

In the evening, when Chen Shimei came back to the residence, he asked the doorman if anyone had come to see him, as he often asked. The man had to tell him that a woman and two children had come and asked for him, announcing that she was his wife. (If he did not let Chen Shimei know this, and Chen Shimei found out about it later, he would be punished or even fired.)

Now, Chen Shimei was frightened. He thought that if the Emperor heard the truth, he could not imagine what result would wait for him. So he sent for Han Qi, a guard in the residence, and told him to go find Qin Xianglian and her two children and kill them. He lied to Han Ji that the woman was his enemy, someone who had always wanted to harm him.

Han Qi did find the woman and the children in the joss house. He did not kill them immediately because he doubted how a woman and two children could harm such a man. He engaged the woman in conversation and asked what the reason Chen Shimei might have for wanting to have them killed. So Qin Xianglian told him the truth. Han Qi flared up. He scorned the man for betraying his wife. So he did not kill them, and on the contrary, he advised her to sue her husband in the yamen of the capital. The mayor of the capital yamen was known by all the people of the city as an upright and just man. He always kept to the law in his judgment of every case, no matter who was involved, even imperial relatives. The mayor was called Bao Zheng, and had a reputation of justice.

When he learned that the imperial son-in-law was being sued, he was not afraid. He only wanted to know the truth. He sat in the public hall where he often tried his cases. He then sent for Chen Shimei, who had to come. If he refused to come, Bao

Zheng would certainly send his yamen police to arrest him. Even the order of the Emperor could not stop him.

In the public hall, when the two children saw Chen Shimei, they cried, "Daddy, we are hungry."

Chen Shimei said, "Who's your daddy?" The boy said, "You."

Qin Xianglian said, "Your honor can send someone to go to Chenjia village in HeNan province. Fetch anyone in the village here to see if the person can recognize him."

This was a fatal blow. Chen Shimei could not deny the accusation anymore. Besides, there was the witness Han Qi, who stated that he had been sent by Chen Shimei to kill the woman and the two children. The crime of Chen Shimei was certain. First, he had committed the crime of sending someone to kill the woman and the two children. Second, he had cheated the Emperor and the princess by not reporting the fact of his marriage. He was sentenced to death.

When the news was known to the princess, she went to see the mayor. Though she understood that her husband had cheated her, she loved the handsome man so much that she did not want him to die; and she did not want to be a widow. She reached the public hall just as the mayor was about to execute Chen Shimei.

When the princess entered the hall, the mayor saluted her and ordered a seat put beside his long table for the princess to sit on. That was a tradition. The princess was only a listener. But she said to the mayor, "You must release him right away. He's my husband." But the mayor did not comply with her. The princess threatened him, saying that she would report to the Emperor. But the mayor said that the law demanded the death sentence for the criminal. So he immediately ordered his yamen policemen to carry out the execution, ignoring the princess.

Chen Shimei was dead and Qin Xianglian returned to her village with her two children. End of story.

CHAPTER 12. HOW DUWEI CAST HER JEWELS AWAY

In the year of 1592, in the Ming Dynasty (1368–1644), Li Jia went to the capital, Beijing, to be enrolled in the government school where students were prepared to pass the government examinations. The eldest son of a high official in the provincial government of Zhenjiang, he was born in Shaoxing city. He had two younger brothers. Arriving in Beijing, Li Jia stayed with another young man called Liu Yuchun who came from the same town. They had studied together and played together. After some time had passed, one day they decided to indulge in a visit to a whorehouse. There was a young girl there, nineteen years of age, renowned in the whole city. She was beautiful and talented, and could sing and play the zither. She had been raised in a good family, but the father fell afoul of the Court. When he died in jail, she was sold to a brothel.

Traditionally, ladies of the evening who were skilled entertainers, able to play the zither or sing for their patrons, play chess, and paint pictures, were sought out for these loftier talents more than the primitive activities commonly associated with such places, although some of their patrons paid higher fees.

Li Jia had brought a lot of money to town with him. He had to live in the capital till the next test session. But as soon as he went out with his friend and met with the famous girl Du Wei, they fell in love with each other. Now, a patron could live with the girl he liked as long as he had money to spend. The house welcomed such patrons. So Li Jia lived with the girl in the brothel for almost a whole year. By degrees, he had less and less money. As a Chinese saying goes: even a mountain of gold will be used up some day. Li Jia could not let his father know that he was living in a whorehouse, and so he could not ask his father for more money. He was penniless now. The madam wanted to expel him from her brothel. She said to Li Jia, "Well, Mister, as you've been away from home so long, I think you should go back home." Li Jia had nothing to say. He had even pawned his spare clothes. The girl knew that the madam was hinting that if Li Jia had nothing more, he had to leave so that the girl could receive other patrons and earn more money for her. The girl had to say that Li Jia was asking his father to send more money here soon.

Du Wei's best chance to make a future for herself was to marry someone who loved her and was reliable. She was well aware of this and had long been looking for a man that she could marry. Now, she had her chance.

Generally, a man who wanted to marry such a girl had to be rich because the redemption for such a skillful and talented working girl was very expensive. It could be as high as 1,000 taels of silver. That was out of the question for Li Jia.

Then Du Wei bargained with her mistress, who was sure that Li Jia could not put down any money. She cut down her demand from 1,000. Finally they struck the deal. If Li Jia could put down 300 taels of silver in the next ten days, he could leave with the girl. After the boss left the room, Du Wei and Li Jia talked the matter over. She wanted the young man to borrow money from relatives and friends in the capital. Li Jia promised to try.

Li Jia knew that he could not borrow money by saying he wanted to redeem a girl from a brothel. None of his relatives or friends would lend him money for such a thing. And if anyone did, his father would surely learn about it. Then the ones who had lent him money would be in trouble with his father, a high official. Therefore, he made up an excuse that he wanted to go home and needed money for the fare. But his relatives and friends had already knew about his misbehavior in a whorehouse. They doubted that this was the real reason why he needed to borrow money. None of them wished to offend his father. So in three days, he was not able to collect any money. He had seven days left. He went to see Liu Yuchun, his roommate. He could tell Liu Yuchun the truth as they both had gone to the brothel.

Generally a girl in this position would not marry a man without money, and Li Jia was destitute now. Liu Yuchun could not believe that the girl would agree to marry him. So Liu Yuchun advised Li Jia to wake up from his sentimental dream and stop borrowing money to redeem her. Without any money, he could not go back to see Du Wei. Therefore, he had to stay with Liu Yuchun and live on the mercy of his friend. Liu Yuchun let him stay without asking him to pay food and board. Thus another three days elapsed. The girl waited and waited without her lover making his appearance. On the seventh day, she sent someone to look for Li Jia and by chance caught him in the street. Li Jia had to go to see Du Wei. When the girl asked him how much money he had borrowed, he made no answer. What could he say? He was ashamed of himself.

Then Du Wei said to him, "I have saved 150 taels of silver. That's the half of the redemption money. You must try to get the other half." So saying, she took out a parcel from a cabinet and handed it to him. Li Jia took the parcel and went to see his friend Liu Yuchun, who was touched by the sincerity of the girl to marry Li Jia, now almost like a beggar. Besides, his father would surely not allow a whore to be his daughter-in-law. So their future was unpredictable. Anyway, Liu Yuchun gave Li Jia the 150 taels of silver out of his own pocket, just intending to help the girl to fulfill her wish.

On the tenth day, Li Jia came and laid down the right amount of silver on the table. The woman had to let the girl go with Li Jia. The other girls came to bid them farewell. One of them gave the girl a small box. Li Jia thought that it might be a gift from the other girls. He did not ask and was not interested to know what was inside it.

Once they made it out, they went to the lodging place of Liu Yuchun to discuss their future. Du Wei said, "We can now travel south, to Suzhou or Hangzhou. I will stay there temporarily and you can go back to see your father. You can find your relatives and get them to persuade your father. If he can forgive you and accept me, you come to fetch me home."

Li Jia said, "It's a good idea. Only I gave all the 300 taels of silver to the woman. We have no money left to travel."

Du Wei produced another package and said, "Here are 50 taels of silver I borrowed from my 'sisters'."

Li Jia took the money and went to hire a coach. They would travel south. They said good-bye to Liu Yuchun and got into the coach, and they left Beijing behind.

They went south and one day came to a river. The river could not take them further south, so they changed for a boat. After two days, they came to Guazhou town and the boat anchored by the wharf. The boatman wanted to go into town to buy provisions. There was another boat tied up to the shore by their boat. A young man sat in that boat, looking out at the town wall. When he saw Li Jia and the girl strolling on the shore, he was stunned to see such a beauty. He was the type of man who was always seducing pretty young girls. Then he deserted them like he was casting away used toothpicks. In order to get acquainted, he greeted Li Jia first, and Li Jia had to return the greeting, according to custom. The man came up to the shore and told Li Jia that his name was Sun Fu and his father was in the salt trade. It meant that he came from a wealthy family.

The next day, strong winds picked up and the boats could not sail. Sun Fu invited Li Jia to his boat to have a drink. Sun Fu intended to lead the conversation to where he wanted it to go. He asked Li Jia about the girl and Li Jia, an honest man, told him everything about himself and the girl. Sun Fu said, "Brother Li, you have made a mess of things. Just think, you spent all the money your father gave you to stay in the capital to study for the tests. Now you spent it all in a brothel. How can you go back to see your father? Besides, will your father accept such a girl as his daughter-in-law? What if your father refuses to take in the girl—where can she go since she's already left that house? Can you harden your heart to betray your father and mother, who need you to take care of them in old age, and desert your parents to go with the girl? If you do so, you will be blamed in scholarly circles."

When Li Jia heard what Sun Fu had said, he knew it was

the truth. He was a well-intentioned man but good for nothing. Generally he could not make up his mind about matters that were of the utmost importance. So he asked Sun Fu to give him some advice. Sun Fu remarked, "If you can listen to me, I will give it. No offense." Li Jia said, "Please."

Sun Fu said, "I will offer you 1,000 taels of silver, and you can take the money to go back to your father. Then your father won't blame you. You, of course, have no need to tell him all the absurdities you did here. And you can leave the girl with me and I will treat her well. You can be sure of it."

Li Jia thought it a good notion. He said, "I'll have to go back and talk it over with her."

When he told Du Wei this, she was devastated; but she did not say anything. What could she say? Finally, she saw through this good-for-nothing man. He could so easily desert the one he had declared he loved so much! She was in despair. But she kept calm.

She said to Li Jia, "Let that man [denoting Sun Fu] bring the silver here and you and he can sign a contract. Then I will go over to his boat and you can go your own way home." This arrangement was agreed upon. When Sun Fu came aboard the boat with the money, the girl brought out her luggage: a small chest with all she had. She stood at the bow of the boat and opened it. For first time, Li Jia saw what was inside. It was full of treasures! There were gold necklaces, bracelets, pearls and precious gems, all the gifts from her patrons over the years, worth far more than the thousand taels of silver. Li Jia was sad, but he stood spellbound. She could have funded their entire future, but wisely had tested his faithfulness first.

On-lookers were gathering on the shore. Everyone had an eye on the stunning box of jewels. They wondered what she was going to do with it. Du Wei drew a last breath and, holding the box in her hands, she dove into the water. The waves carried her away downstream and she was gone.

Well, Li Jia returned home safely, but he began to suffer from schizophrenia. Sun Fu later often dreamed of the ghost of the girl coming to demand that he give her back her life. He died soon afterwards.

Liu Yuchun, the roommate of Li Jia in Beijing, started to travel south, too. He was going home. He took a boat downstream and one night after the death of the girl, he dreamed of her, telling him that she had left him something in return for his kindly lending money to Li Jia. Next day, he found a wooden chest in the mud along the shore. He climbed down to the riverbank and picked it up. He heaved a deep and sorrowful sigh, though he made a fortune.

CHAPTER 13. HOW THE OIL PEDDLER WOOED A COURTESAN

Families separated in the chaos of war

In the Northern Song Dynasty, in a village outside the capital city Bianliang, there lived a well-to-do family of three. They owned a shop selling the miscellaneous staples of life—rice, wheat, cooking oil, salt, wine, tea, and everything else for the household. The father was named Xin Shan, the wife was Yuan, and the daughter was Yaoqin—a clever and beautiful girl. She went to lessons with the boys in the village school. At the age of ten, she could write poems and essays. By the age of twelve, she was learning how to play the zither and chess. She was also showing talent as a painter.

That year when she was twelve, the Jin tribe, a minority in the north, invaded the territory of the Northern Song. They robbed and killed wherever they went. People inside and outside the city fled southward, and so did the Xin family.

The defeated government soldiers were as bad off as the townsfolk, their supply chain being disrupted, and they had no more food. So they robbed the refugees as they ran away from the enemy to the south. Parents and children of many families got separated as they all fled in panic, running here and there for dear life. And so Yaoqin was separated from her parents.

She ran and ran as long as she could, and then, being exhausted, looked for some shelter where she might rest. She saw a little hut by the roadside that appeared to be deserted. She went inside and leaned back against the wall to rest. Just then, in came a man from the same village where she had lived with her parents. He was called Bu Qiao, and he recognized the girl. Yaoqin knew him too, and asked for help. So Bu Qiao took her along with him toward the south, saying that he would look for her parents. On the way, he warned her that they had better pretend to be father and daughter, or people might think that he kidnapped the girl.

The Jin, who had originated with the nomadic tribes of Central Asia, occupied the region north of the Yangtze River. They lived in tents, not in houses like the Han tribe that formed the majority population in China. When the Jin occupied the capital, they captured the Emperor and hustled him off to the north.

But one of the Emperor's sons had escaped south, accompanied by many courtiers. They crossed the Yangtze River and reached Hangzhou city, which was known as a center for silk production, printing, and brewing industry. They made it the new capital, and historians considered this the establishment of the Southern Song Dynasty, as it was south of the river.

Hangzhou is a large city and at that time, in 1129, it was renamed LinAn, "Temporary Peace." In an unusual fashion, the city of LinAn was arranged so that it all was oriented toward the north, looking back toward the land they wished to reclaim. Many refugees rushed there because one could make a living, either in the big city or in the vicinity.

The man Bu Qiao and the girl Yaoqin entered the city, too. Bu Qiao was not an entirely honorable man. He was taking the girl along with the intention of selling her to a whorehouse so that he could get a lot of money. In the city he found a big whorehouse and talked to the madam (behind the back of the girl). They struck a bargain for fifty silver taels. Then Bu Qiao told Yaoqin she could stay there as it was the home of one of his relatives. "And from here I'll go to find your parents. Then we will come to get you."

Yaoqin was too young to know about such things, and she was so relieved to have shelter and food that she did not immediately perceive that there were peculiar goings on. At any rate, she was under-age, and not until she reached 15 that could she be used to receive patrons. Pretty as she was and talented as well, the calculation was that she would make a top tier "escort" and would be highly profitable to the house when the time came. So the madam treated her well.

But when she reached the age of 15, the madam had to make sure Yaoqin understood that, indeed, this was a brothel and she was not a guest but a courtesan, and she would have to receive patrons. When the girl realized how profoundly she had been deceived and her trust abused, she began to cry bitterly. She refused to receive any men.

Generally, a girl in a brothel who was not willing to work would be beaten or whipped till she complied. But then there was the risk of bruising, even scarring and disfiguring the body; that would reduce her value. So no one could beat Yaoqin, because she was too precious to be left with any marks.

As a rule in that business, when a new girl was approaching the legal age, a frequent patron of the house would be given the privilege of taking away her maidenhood. Some rich men liked virgins in particular. But for this, a patron should pay much more than he did when he engaged with one of the girls who was not a virgin. And such patrons were always wealthy men. They did not mind paying extra for the rare opportunity. Now the woman in charge called in her friend, an old woman called Liu SiNiang, and together they worked out a plot. One day when a rich patron called Jin Er came in. He wanted to have a virgin. So the madam asked Yaoqin to play zither for the patron and said that after that she could go back to her own room, which meant no love-making between her and the patron. Yaoqin thought it would be no harm, and so she agreed.

The patron ordered some food and wine. He kept inviting Yaoqin to drink (insisting, even), and she could not refuse. Pretty soon Yaoqin was so drunk that she was laid down on her own bed and the patron simply raped her. The next morning when she woke up, she came to realize what had happened to her. She wept for her sorrowful fate. She locked her door would not let anyone come in. She did not wish to see anyone right now. The brothel-keeper knocked at her door, but she just lay on her bed and said nothing. The brothel-keeper was at her wits' end. She sent for her friend Liu SiNiang for assistance.

Liu SiNiang went to knock at the door, saying, "Yaoqin, it's me, your auntie. I've come to comfort you." She was always nice to Yaoqin, who now felt that she couldn't shut her out. So she got up and opened the door. Liu SiNiang stepped in and they chatted for a while. She tried to persuade the girl to go along with things, reasoning that if Yaoqin refused to receive visitors, she would be beaten, then deprived of food, and eventually just be bound hand and foot and the results would be the same. Besides, if her parents were found, and she was badly injured by then or had even died, what would her parents do?

By this means, she was forced to receive patrons. Since she had such fine qualities, she had admirers among the richest men and she became well-known round the city.

How the oil peddler met Yaoqin

There was a poor family, a father and son, living in another village outside the capital city. The mother had died before the raiders from the north came down; the father and son ran away to the south together. When they reached LinAn city, the father thought that since he had no way to support his son, he would have to leave him with another family. They came upon an oil shop owned by Zhu Shilao, who had no son of his own; his wife had died early. So he took in the boy and treated him like his own son. The father then went to a temple to become a monk.

The boy was named Qin Chong. The oil shop flourished but the old man was beginning to suffer declining health. They hired another man as assistant, who was called Xing Quan. Four years had passed since Qin Chong had joined Zhu Shilao. He was now seventeen. Old Zhu Shilao had a maid who waited on them. By now, the maid had grown up, too. As the boy was handsome, she liked him; but she was ugly and older than he was. He could not return her feelings.

Therefore, the maid turned her attention to the assistant, Xing Quan, who was just at the right age to marry. So they got together and made a plan. First, they thought, they should drive away young Qin Chong and then, when the old man died, they could take over the shop as their own property.

The maid kicked off their scheme by slandering the boy to the old man. The maid said that Qin Chong was stealing money from shop's till. Then she told the old man that Qin Chong was continually flirting with her. Surprisingly, old man drove his adopted son away without even investigating the truth of the stories, giving him only three taels of silver to live on.

Qin Chong left the shop and searched for a place to live. Finally he found some small hovel in another part of town and he rented it. Then he bought two buckets filled with oil and a thick stick to use as a yoke to carry the two buckets. He shouldered the burden and went round the city to sell the oil. Back when he had been working in the oil shop, many people in the area came to buy oil there because they saw that he was an honest young man. Now he was selling oil as a peddler, they all came to him to buy their oil.

So Qin Chong was gradually able to save up some money. And once, he came upon a temple, weighed down with his wares, just when the temple needed more oil for the lamps before the Buddha. The monks liked him and asked him to bring them oil on a regular basis. At the base of the temple there was a big house, and that is where the brothel was where Yaoqin was trapped. When Qin Chong was passing by, the madam went out to buy oil from him, too. Then she also asked him to make regular deliveries.

Some of the brothel's patrons would ask the girls to go out with them, especially Yaoqin. They would take Yaoqin for a boat ride on the famous West Lake in Hangzhou. Later in the evening, they would walk her back to the whorehouse. So sometimes the oil peddler would see the girl. She was so beautiful. Qin Chong was stunned at the sight of such a lovely young woman, and he thought that she would be the girl he wanted for his wife. He felt pity that such a beautiful girl was stuck as a courtesan. He wished to deliver her from such a fate.

One day when Qin Chong came to sell his oil at the whorehouse, he and the madam had a chat. He asked how much a patron would pay for one night's stay, and he learned that the fee was ten silver taels.

Now Qin Chong began to save his money in earnest, and after a few years he had sixteen silver taels. If he spent ten taels, he would still have six taels left for the business. That was enough. So he went to see the madam to ask for one night's stay with Yaoqin. She was certainly surprised to know that such a poor boy was prepared to spend so much money, and for such an extravagance. She advised him, "You'd better save the money for your business. Why squander it this way?" But the young man insisted, saying that it was his life's desire to get acquainted with the girl. So the madam said that she would arrange for him to meet her. "I think you can come in the evening, two days from now."

Qin Chong was happy and waited impatiently for two long days. On the third day, he took a day off from selling oil and went to buy new clothes. A man's robe at that time had a special style. Its sleeves were long and wide. The end of the sleeve was sewed up to leave an opening for the hand to stick out. And the sewed-up part of the sleeve was use as a pocket; one could keep money or anything else in it.

Qin Chong arrived in the evening a bit early and was asked to sit in the girl's room. The girl had suddenly been asked away by a patron; and when she got back, she was drunk. She had to be helped to her room and to lie down on her bed. It looked like the girl could not even talk with him. His money was wasted that evening. But he did not regret it. He sat beside the bed patiently and silently. At midnight the girl seemed to revive a little. She wanted to vomit. Qin Chong could not find any container to hold it, and so he held up his sleeve and let her vomit into it. Now his new gown was soiled, so he took it off and bundled it up, intending to wash it when returning home.

The next morning Yaoqin was fully awake and got a good look at Qin Chong. When she saw him, she asked what had actually happened the night before. He was straightforward and quite ingenuous in his telling of the story. Now, the girl was deeply moved. All the patrons took her just for a plaything. Only this young man treated her as a soul mate. If she could marry such a reliable person, her life would be worth living. But just now, he had to leave, as it was morning and the rules required that he depart.

Now let's go back to the oil shop and see how things were

developing there. Business went on as usual for a brief time, and then one evening, the maid and the assistant took all the money from the shop and eloped together.

The old man was appalled, and especially he regretted allowing such people to convince him to drive away his adopted son. He asked a neighbor if he could help him find his son and ask him to come back to the shop. The neighbor knew it would be easy to find the young man, as almost everyone in the neighborhood was still buying oil from him. Qin Chong was a gold-hearted boy and when he heard that the old man was asking for him, he immediately returned to the shop to see his adoptive father. The old man was overjoyed, and let Qin Chong run the shop.

Years later, when the old man died, the son did come to own the shop. He began to sell other necessities besides oil, and he became well-to-do. Now he needed help. So he put up a notice on the shop door. One day a man, middle-aged, came to ask for the job. He looked like he was a good man, and so he was employed. When he was invited to bring all his belongings and move here, he mentioned that he had a wife still in the lodging place. Qin Chong had him bring his wife too. So the couple lived in the shop, helping to sell things. The man was Xin Shan, the father of Yaoqin, separated ever since their desperate flight before the Jin raiders.

For these few years, Yaoqin had gone on living as she had to do. Then an incident occurred. A young man named Wu Ba, whose father was a mayor in another city, was arrogant and used to acting with impunity wherever he went. He had a very poor reputation and was known for bad conduct. Now, he had been hearing for a long time about this famous beauty. And Yaoqin had long heard of this scoundrel, too, and knew his bad repute. One day, he came to the whorehouse and demanded to see her. But she put her foot down and refused. He became furious and dashed to her room with his servants. The door was locked. He bade his servants to break open the door and pull the girl out. He took her by force to his boat on the lake. The madam could do nothing to help her. She could not even report it to the yamen because his father was a high official.

The boat was rowed far away from the brothel, and then he had his men dump the delicate girl on the shore and leave her to see what her destiny would be, if she was so haughty that she would not receive the son of a mayor.

And he and his boat went off. Yaoqin could not walk such a long way back. Her feet were bound—they were tiny and could not bear much weight; she really could not walk far at all.

So what was her destiny, then, indeed? Qin Chong had just gone to a temple in this area to worship Buddha and was now on his way back home. Here he was, walking along the shore, and by chance he saw the girl. He hired a boat to escort her back to the whorehouse.

After this incident, Yaoqin was afraid that such things would happen to her again. The madam was afraid, too. The girl determined to quit the job and marry some good and reliable man. Then she recalled the oil peddler who had been so tender and kind. She asked Liu SiNiang to seek him out, and not long after, she found him. Qin Chong came to see her, and he happily agreed they should marry. Yaoqin had saved up enough money to redeem herself, as wealthy patrons traditionally would give such a famous girl a handsome gift on the first night to soften her up and also make her happy to welcome him the next time he visited. So Yaoqin spoke with the madam and purchased her freedom.

Then Yaoqin went with Qin Chong to the oil shop, where the old couple came out to welcome the new bride. They were almost paralyzed with shock and disbelief. Here was their long lost daughter! And she recognized her parents, too. So the family was united, beyond any hopes, after so many years of separation and in a strange city.

CHAPTER 14. THE TALE OF JIN YUNU AND HER HUSBAND

A suitable husband

There lived in Hangzhou city a family named Jin. The father, Old Jin, was the chief of the beggars in this area. As the beggars' chief, he did not need to go out begging himself. He stayed home and all other beggars had to bring a certain percentage of their gains to him. He was a kind of king in his territory. In fact, he had amassed a fortune. Still, he was a beggar in name, and this affected his daughter's prospects for marriage. She aspired to marry a scholar (a class of people that once were highly esteemed), and scholars mostly came from families who would never let their sons marry the daughter of a beggar, no matter how much wealth he had set by. Family reputation was of paramount importance.

Old Jin's daughter was named Jin Yunu, and she was already eighteen years old. In ancient China, fifteen was the right age for most girls to get married. The Jin family were just these two: father and daughter. The mother had died early. As Old Jin was wealthy, his daughter had received a good education. She could write poems and essays, and could play the zither and the fife. She was as well-endowed and accomplished as the daughters of other rich families.

That winter, it snowed heavily. Even the beggars would not go out. The beggars, like the squirrels, had something in store for the winter season. Only lazy beggars who failed to stock up would risk being frozen to death by the roadside.

Now a young man came along, plodding through the snow. His clothes did not look like a beggar's. When he reached the door of the Jins' house, it seemed that his legs could no longer support his body, and he fell to the ground. His body banged against the door of the house. Jin Yunu was sewing, sitting close to the door. When she heard the sound of a heavy weight falling on the door, she went to open it. A young man fell in. He had fainted.

Jin Yunu called her father, not knowing what to do. Old Jin rushed to see, and concluded that the young man had fainted from hunger. He might not have eaten anything for one or two days. Besides, his thin clothes were entirely inadequate to the cold. The father carried the young man, helped by the daughter, into a bedroom. They laid him on the bed. Jin Yunu went to kitchen to prepare some hot porridge to warm him up while the father pricked the man's philtrum (the groove that runs from the nose to the upper lip) with his thumb nail of his right hand. Chinese people believe that this will make a fainting person recover his senses. So the man opened his eyes. He looked around, trying to figure out where he was. His last memory was that of falling in front of a door. Presently, the girl came in with a hot bowl of porridge. She fed it to the man, who was still weak and had to accept the favor of being fed by an unknown girl—and a really a beautiful girl, at that. (Have you noticed that young girls in every story are beautiful?)

As he finished the porridge, he felt somewhat recovered. He got up from the bed and sat on a chair at the table. He understood that both the old man and girl were waiting for him to tell them his story. His name was Mo Ji. He lived in a village not too far away. His parents had died when he was still a little boy. A paternal relative took care of him. He was sent to the village school to get an education, and now he wanted to go to the capital to take government tests. The relative had even given him a bit of money, but he was only a peasant and did not have much to give. Thus the young man had set out on foot. Even so, his food money was already spent and indeed, he had not eaten for two days. He had no strength to go on.

The girl began to like this man as he looked like a scholar, the type she liked. Later, when she and her father were alone in another room, she hinted to her father about it. Her father considered that it was not going to be easy for his daughter to finally find a man she liked, at the age of eighteen. He went to talk to the man and asked him if he had a wife. The answer was, of course, negative, or we wouldn't have much of a story. Anyway, how could such a poor man have a wife? So the father said, "You are still single, and my daughter likes you. What would you think about marrying?" Well, the man thought what any poor man would think—a lovely girl, plus room and board. He agreed straight off.

Then a wedding was held and the neighbors were invited to celebrate. There were also some tables set for beggars. Thus, the bridegroom came to find out that his father-in-law was the chief of the beggars. But he didn't say a thing, and he didn't show any sign of his dissatisfaction. At least he had a wife now.

After several days spent in celebrating the marriage, Jin Yunu urged her husband to review his books so that he could to go the capital the next year as planned and take the government tests. Her ambition was still to have a husband who was a government official, so that she could become a lady.

A suitable bride

The next autumn, in the year when the government tests would be held, Mo Ji bade adieu to his wife and his father-in-law. The wife gave him plenty of money to spend on the way and while he was in the capital.

There was another young student living in the same neighborhood and so they traveled together. This young man, by the name of Li Ao, knew everything about Mo Ji. When they arrived in the capital, they stayed in the same inn. There were quite a few test-takers lodging there. Li Ao was a person who liked to joke around, not always caring if he hurt someone's feelings. So, he told the other test-takers, with a chuckle, that Mo Ji was the son-in-law of the chief of the beggars. Someone laughed at Mo Ji for that. Mo Ji was so embarrassed that he moved to another inn.

After the tests, the notice of the results was posted on the wall. Mo Ji had passed, and he was named to a government office at last. He was a petty official, but that was better than nothing. He was assigned a position in a small town. Usually, the scholars would go home first to let their family and relatives know the happy news before moving to take up their new positions. They were allowed a few days off as vacation.

When Mo Ji got back to his wife's house, Yunu was joyful. She actually had a husband who was an official. Neighbors came to celebrate.

After a few days, Mo Ji had to start on his way to his work place. Generally, in such a case, the man would take his wife or family to the new location. So he and his wife hired a boat to take them to the assigned town, and they set off on their journey.

One evening, their boat anchored at a wharf close to a village for the night. Mo Ji looked at his wife in the cabin, and he suddenly recalled Li Ao's disdain as he laughed at him over his father-in-law's social status. He felt ashamed. Then he made a decision. He could get rid of this wife and marry another, someone whose family had a better reputation. He beckoned his wife to come out of the cabin to the bow of the boat. When she was standing beside him, he suddenly pushed her into the water and told the boatmen to set sail immediately. As his boat pulled away, another boat came to anchor there.

When Yunu was pushed into the water, she struggled and cried for help. In the second boat there was an older couple. The husband was going to the small town to serve as mayor there. When he heard the cry for help, he told his boatman to save the young woman. Jin Yunu was pulled up into his boat. After she recovered a little, the old couple asked her what had happened. The couple were outraged and wanted to punish the heartless husband. The old couple, who had no children of their own, felt a great sympathy for Yunu and they adopted her as their daughter.

Not long after, they arrived at the destination. As fate would have it, Mo Ji worked in the yamen of this town, precisely under the new mayor. When the mayor learned who this Mo Ji was, working in his yamen, he told Yunu. She wanted to avenge herself on the heartless husband, and she was struck with a wonderful idea.

One day, the mayor summoned Mo Ji to his office. When they both were seated, the mayor asked Mo Ji, "Do you have a wife?" Mo Ji replied, "No."

The mayor said, "I have a daughter. As you are a promising young man, I'd like to give you the hand of my daughter in marriage. What do you think?" Mo Ji was, of course, delighted. So the wedding was arranged.

On the wedding night, when the ceremony and eating and drinking were done, the bridegroom was led into the wedding chamber. According to tradition, the bride was sitting on the edge of the bed, with two maids standing beside her. The bride was covered with a veil over her head, in red, the color for good fortune. But good fortune for whom? By tradition, the bridegroom was supposed to lift the red veil now, and only then did he get to see what his bride looked like.

This time, events did not unfold entirely according to tradition. As soon as he entered the room, the two maids began beating him with sticks. He was baffled and asked what why they were doing that. No one answered, and the maids only smacked him harder. He began to cry "Help! Help!" The bride took off the red veil herself and showed her face. As Mo Ji set his eyes upon the face of his new wife, he cried "Ghost!" in fright.

The mayor came in at this moment and told him just what had happened. Mo Ji fell on his knees to beg forgiveness from his former wife and new wife. Yunu forgave him, at last, after punishing him like this. And now Mo Ji was satisfied because his wife was the daughter of a mayor, while her husband was launched in his career as an official.

CHAPTER 15. LI SHISHI AND THE EMPEROR

The story happened in the capital of the Northern Song Dynasty. Wang Shishi (1062–1129), a very beautiful girl, was the daughter of Wang Yin, who owned a dye shop. When she was four years of age, her father fell afoul of the authorities and was put into jail, where he died. The daughter was adopted by Li Yun, who owned a whorehouse. So Wang Shishi's name was changed to Li Shishi. As she was growing up, she was taught all sorts of skills that a courtesan needed to please her patrons and get money out of their pockets.

A talented courtesan could become quite renowned and attract many visitors. As many well-known courtesans in the history of China were skilled in poetry and painting, many men of letters came to visit them from all over the country, men who were famous poets or painters themselves. They did not come primarily for love-making. They would discuss how to write poems, or how to play the zither. They might just drink tea and talk about learned matters. Thus, among the visitors of Li Shishi were such famous men of letters.

Zhang Xian (990–1078) was a famous poet and the mayor of Anlu town. He was nicknamed "Three Shadows," because he had written three well-known poetic sentences with the word shadow in each of them:

"Clouds break, the moon shows, the flowers play with
the shadow."

"The screen rolls up the flower shadow."

"Catkins fall without shadow."

Yan Jidao (1038–1110) was a high official. He and his father
Yan Shu (991–1055) were both famous poets. An anthology of
his poems has been handed down to us through history.

Qin Guan (1049–1100) was appointed an editor to compile
the official compendium of history of that time. He was also a
famous poet and essayist.

Zhou Bangyan (1056–1121) was the mayor of Lishui town and
later was promoted to be the head of the music academy in the
palace. He was just six years older than Li Shishi, and so he was
closer to her than were her other visitors, and she liked him better than others.

Her visitors also included two courtiers, Gao Qiu and Wang
Fu. Gao Qiu was a favorite courtier of the Emperor Huizong.
Gradually, through Gao Qiu, the Emperor came to know the
name of Li Shishi. In the end, the Emperor wanted the two courtiers to take him to see this talented girl. The emperor was greatly
attracted by her beauty and disposition. That night he stayed in
her bedroom, and in the early hours of the morning the Emperor
quickly put on his clothes and hurried back in time for the levée.

When the two courtiers brought the Emperor in, they did
not make any introduction. So Li Shishi did not really know who
the man was. However, by degrees, she began to suspect that
this man must be the Emperor because the two courtiers paid
him so much respect. Of course, she wisely pretended that she
did not know this.

Once the Emperor had stayed with Li Shishi, he never
touched his concubines any more. They were nothing compared
with her. It was no wonder. The concubines in the palace did
everything by ceremony. If by any chance one of them infringed
any palace regulation, she would be punished. Therefore, the
concubines were very self conscious and controlled in their
words and actions, cautious and restrained. They did not even
dare to tell jokes for fear of inadvertently offending the Emperor.

But for Li Shishi, she could act freely. She could even joke with the Emperor, as she pretended not to know who he was. She treated him like an ordinary person. So he felt relaxed with her, and their interactions were warmer than his usual experience. As Emperor, he could never act freely or he would incur criticism from people, which would mar his reputation. He finally had a tunnel made from his palace directly to her room so that he could come and go without anyone else detecting it. Although he could not come every day, as this information leaked out, other potential visitors began to stay away since no one dared to get into trouble with the Emperor.

There were two exceptions. Once Zhou Bangyan came, in the daytime, thinking that the Emperor was not free at that hour. He had not seen the girl in a long time. But unexpectedly, the Emperor came through the tunnel right after the levée. Zhou Bangyan had to hide under the bed till the Emperor left.

The second person was Song Jiang, who was the leader of the rebels on Mt. Liang in Shandong province. He had thirty-six sworn brothers and thousand of rebel fighters. There was a lake round the mountain so that the government army had difficulties to wipe out the rebels. But as a matter of fact, they did not want to rebel. They were forced by corrupt local officials and officers. The rebels really wanted to capitulate. As Song Jiang was reported that the Emperor often went to see Li Shishi, he wanted to get in touch through the girl with the Emperor to talk over how they could capitulate and turn over to the government.

At that time there was war between the government and the Jin tribe in the north who had invaded during the Northern Song Dynasty. Li Shishi had saved a lot of money given by her patrons. Now, as the war broke out, she donated all her money for the military expenses of the government.

In 1125, Emperor Huizong gave up the throne and let his son Qinzong take his place. He himself just enjoyed the leisure and did what he liked. But soon after, Jin tribe came to conquer the capital and capture the two emperors, father and son. They both were taken north to the territory of the Jin. The Jin commander wanted to capture Li Shishi, too, but in that he failed. Her renown had spread so far and wide, even the leader of the Jin tribe wanted her.

Li Shishi had the good fortune to escape to the south, but after such a grand life, the rest does not sound so fortunate after all. It was said that she toured for some time in Zhejiang province and made her living by singing for rich people; finally, after all the admiration and distinction, she died in poverty.

CHAPTER 16. THE COURTESAN WHO CHANGED THE HISTORY OF THE MING DYNASTY

How to breach the strongest defense

It was round the end of the Ming Dynasty (1368–1644). Emperor Chongzhen was on the throne. When he first became the Emperor, he had the ambition to make his empire strong, but he was not a man of talent, and the empire remained weak. In northeastern China there were the Mandarin, who got stronger and stronger, especially when they united with the Mongolians in the west. Now they intended to invade and occupied the territory of the Ming Dynasty. The only obstruction to them was the Great Wall. They would have to enter through Shanhai Pass at the eastern end of the Great Wall.

The Ming Dynasty stationed great forces there to defend it. But the Emperor was short-sighted and often changed the commander, which created a disadvantageous situation for the defending army. Every time a commander had gotten familiar with the situation and began to be able to interpret the moves of the enemy, on which he would base his strategy, he was removed and a new commander would be sent in. The new commander needed time to get familiar with everything over again.

First the Emperor appointed the famous General Yuan

Chonghuan (1584–1630) as commander at the pass. He defeated the Mandarin army a few times, and they had to retreat. Then the Mandarins sent spies to the capital of the Ming Dynasty to spread a rumor that Yuan Chonghuan was holding peace talks with the Mandarins. The emperor was dead set on driving the Mandarins back to where they came from, so there was no peace to discuss and nothing to negotiate. Therefore, the Emperor summoned Yuan Chonghuan back and put him to death for treason.

Then he appointed Hong Chengchou (1593–1665) as the commander. He was a wise courtier and was the minister of the Military Ministry. When the Mandarins heard about the removal of Yuan Chonghuan, they marched their army towards Shanhai Pass again. Hong Chengchou wanted to show that he was able and fearless, but in the first battle, he was captured. He was presented to the Mandarin emperor Huangtaiji (1592–1643), who tried to persuade Hong to turn over to their side. At first, Hong Chengchou refused to betray his emperor. According to the historical record, one night Hong Chengchou woke up at midnight and found a woman lying beside him. He sat up in astonishment and asked who she was. The woman said that she was the empress of Huangtaiji; she had come to sleep with him. This was a great honor to him. He was so moved that he surrendered. It is said that he kowtowed only to the empress, not to the Emperor, saying that he was her slave. The emperor did not care about that, as long as he had surrendered to the Mandarin. Hong Chengchou then offered quite a few ideas on how to conquer the Ming Dynasty.

After Hong Chengchou was captured, Emperor Chongzhen appointed Wu SanGui as the next commander.

Wu SanGui and Chen Yuanyuan

Chen Yuanyuan lived in Kunshan town in Jiangsu province, south of the Yangtze River. She was the most celebrated courtesan in that area. Many patrons came to hear her sing and watch her dance.

At that time large peasant revolts were breaking out, rebelling against the oppression by corrupt officials. Their leader was Li Zicheng (1606–1645). Li Zicheng led a huge army of rebels marching towards the capital, Beijing. Facing both a threat from the Mandarins and from internal rebels, the Emperor felt so heavyhearted and melancholy that he was practically ill. One of his imperial concubines, Tian, wanted to cheer him up. She asked her father Tian Hong to find some more beautiful girls. It was believed at the time that the most beautiful girls were in region south of the Yangtze River. Tian Hong thereby traveled south, and he visited brothel after brothel until at last he found Chen Yuanyuan in Kunshan town. He was struck by her beauty and took her back to the capital. He spent 200,000 silver taels for her. He presented the girl to the Emperor, but for once he was in no mood for singing and dancing. Tian Hong had to take the girl back to his own residence.

Commander Wu SanGui went with his army to Shanhai Pass to repel the Mandarin invasion. He went through the capital and Tian Hong entertained him, hoping that Wu would especially protect his family and his fortune. He let Chen Yuanyuan dance for Wu SanGui, who fell for her at first sight. He told Tian Hong that he would try his best to protect him—if he gave him the girl. Of course, Tian Hong complied. Wu SanGui took her to his residence in the capital. But when he left the capital for the frontier, he had to leave the girl behind.

How the Mandarin established their Qing Dynasty

Li Zicheng's rebel army approached the capital. The Emperor did not have enough troops to defend the city, and soon the rebels broke in. The Emperor had to hang himself. That was the end of the Ming Dynasty. Li Zicheng occupied the palace and declared himself emperor of the Dashun Empire. One of his generals, Liu Zongming, killed all the family members of Wu SanGui and took the girl with him.

When Wu SanGui heard the news, he was infuriated and vowed to take revenge on the rebels. He knew that the forces he commanded were still no match for the great numbers of the rebel army. Finally he had to ally with the Mandarins and used the allied force to fight the rebels. Thus, the Mandarin army entered the Shanhai Pass and then occupied the territory of Ming Dynasty. They founded their Qing Dynasty till overthrown by the Republic of China in 1911.

The rebels escaped from the capital Beijing. Wu SanGui chased them till he wiped out all the rebels. In pursuit of the defeated rebels, Wu SanGui came across Chen Yuanyuan. When Wu got back his girl, he marched into Yunnan province, in the far southwest corner of China. He made it his own territory. He was given the title of king and Yunnan province as his fiefdom by the Emperor of the Qing Dynasty. He accepted the title.

As time proceeded, Chen Yuanyuan began to show her age, and Wu SanGui's attention shifted to some younger girls. Chen Yuanyuan went to live in a Buddhist nunnery for a quiet life.

Although We SanGui had let in the Mandarin army, he did it just for his own purpose. He was no real friend of the Mandarin, after all. He wished to be independent. So he declared that his fief in Yunnan province was an independent empire and was no longer a subject of the Qing Dynasty. He set Kunming city as his capital.

The Qing government dispatched troops into Yunnan province to attack him and they conquered Kunming. Wu SanGui was killed. Chen Yuanyuan was afraid she would be captured by the Qing army and humiliated; she drowned herself in the lotus pond outside the nunnery. She was buried by the side of the pond. In the nunnery two pictures of Chen Yuanyuan are displayed.

If Chen Yuanyuan never lived, or if Wu SanGui had never met her, he would not have allowed in the Mandarin and the Ming Dynasty might have continued for a longer time. Even if the rebels had occupied the capital, the deceased emperor had sons; and one of those sons could have gathered troops from other provinces and driven off the rebels. Perhaps the Ming Dynasty would have been restored. That's why people said it was a whore that changed the history of the Ming Dynasty.

CHAPTER 17. THE TALE OF ESQUIRE YANG AND SWEET CABBAGE

This story happened under the reign of Empress Dowager Cixi in the late Qing Dynasty. Esquire Yang lived in Yuhang town of Zhejiang Province. He had passed two government tests and had been given an honorary title; but he didn't apply for an official post. His family was rich. He enjoyed studying herbal medicine, and sometimes he served the neighborhood as a doctor. Across the street from his house there was a tofu shop, run by a husband and wife who made bean curd.

The wife was beautiful and was called by the nickname "Cabbage" because her complexion was fair (not tanned and lined from working in the fields) and she was plump and juicy. Esquire Yang and the husband and wife were well acquainted, since they were close neighbors.

Liu, the mayor of the town, had an indolent son whose only interests were women and loading around. No studying for him; no serious endeavor at all. But he was young and handsome. He devoted most of his creative energies to chasing girls or visiting with prostitutes.

One day the son happened to pass the bean curd shop and saw the wife Little Cabbage, who was talking to the customers and packing up their bean curd for them. He halted before the shop, fixing his eyes on her face. When the other customers left, he was still standing there, spellbound. A simple girl, she didn't suspect anything but asked him politely, "How can I help you, Customer?"

A practiced seducer, he stepped forward, pretending that he wanted to buy from her. But instead of talking like a customer, he introduced himself, saying, "I am the son of the mayor." Often, when people heard that, they would stand in awe of him. That was just the effect he wished.

Cabbage was awed, too. She apologized for not recognizing him and then she begged to know how much bean curd he wanted.

But he only asked, flirtingly, "How old are you, little Beauty?" Cabbage lowered her eyes and coyly smiled.

The son asked, "Are you married?"

Cabbage replied this time, "Yes, I am." She hoped that he would leave, now, since she was married.

Nevertheless, the son said, "If you marry me, you'll live comfortably and happily all your life." (He knew that that was impossible. His mayor father would never assent to his marrying "with the left hand." He only said it as a temptation. Anything, to get close to her.

And that was all. The husband showed up, and he had to leave.

From then on, the mayor's son often came to the shop, but he never bought any bean curd. When the husband was out, he flirted with Cabbage, teased her, importuned her, even threatened her. Some women are vain by nature; some are too timid to tell a man to go away. The son would bring her gifts: cosmetics and expensive clothes. At first Cabbage refused to accept anything from him, but he would just leave the things behind in the shop and go his merry way. Cabbage had to hide these gifts that were forced upon her, making sure her husband would not see them. By degrees, she came to accept the attentions of this handsome young man, the son of the mayor. And finally she gave in to his pleadings.

However, the son wasn't even discrete. He didn't keep their adultery a secret, as he should have done. He was actually boastful of his conquests and knew he could act with impunity, since no one dared to offend the son of the mayor.

Her husband soon came to hear of it, but what could he do? He could not sue the son in his own father's yamen. On the contrary, the son was jealous of the husband and decided to get rid of him.

One chilly day, the husband was taken ill. Cabbage went across the street to Esquire Yang for medical advice and asked him to come over to see her husband. Esquire Yang followed her into the bedroom in the back of the shop. Yang saw that the husband must have simply caught cold, and he prescribed some medical herbs and minerals, and left. Cabbage got ready to go and buy the medicine, but just then the son arrived. Hearing that the husband was sick and that she was on her way to the drugstore, he offered to go in her stead.

Off he went, and duly purchased all the medicines on the prescription. Then, as if suddenly remembering an errand of his own, he asked for a small packet of arsenic "to poison the mice in my house." Back at the tofu shop, he gave all the small packets to Cabbage, and quickly departed. At first, Cabbage thought there was one extra packet, but she decided that she must have misremembered and that all these powders must have been on Yang's list. She put everything together in a pot to simmer. When the medicine was ready, she poured it into a bowl; after it cooled a little, she helped her husband to sip it. He drank it down. Before long, the husband cried out in pain and began to thrash around on the bed. Cabbage did not know what to do; she just watched. In the next moment, blood came out from his nose and mouth. Poisoned! Cabbage suddenly remembered the extra little packet, but it was too late to mention it now.

In such a case, the wife would have to report to the government. So a coroner came, and detected a trace of arsenic. He reported it to the mayor and of course, the wife was arrested as a suspect. The mayor's son hadn't thought of that. Things were getting out of hand.

He went to the jail to visit Cabbage, who complained that he had destroyed her life.

"It's no use to blame me," He said. "There is no evidence against me. I have come to rescue you."

"How?"

"As of now, you are only a suspect. If you can name someone

else as the culprit, you will be released." The son had no brains for any useful work, but he was full of clever ideas for luring people astray, making trouble, and lying his way out of things. He still found Cabbage pleasant to be with and wanted to save her life. He knew that they'd have to find a scapegoat, or the case couldn't be closed.

"But there isn't anyone," she sobbed.

"Who wrote you the prescription?"

"Esquire Yang." The son knew him — in fact, he hated him, for his learning.

The mayor often drew unflattering comparisons between his son and Yang, and

scolded him for neglecting his studies. So the son said, "Yang's the one."

"No, he's a nice man. We've been friends since childhood. I can't involve him in this."

"Then, you will die." The law was very simple: Anyone who kills must be executed. "Please, do it for me," said the son. "When you are released, we'll go somewhere else and live together. Besides, Yang won't be executed — he has an honorary title. At the worst, he will be deprived of his title. This time." Cabbage knew nothing of the law, and believed him. By this time, she had begun to love this man, and she was eager to believe in his vision of a life together. Especially now that her husband had died.

A few days later, Cabbage was brought before the mayor to be interrogated. "How did you murder your husband?"

"I didn't murder my husband. There's been a mistake," she replied, on her knees.

"If you didn't do it, then who did?" The mayor sounded fierce.

"I don't know. Not me." Her voice was so low that the mayor barely heard her. He ordered the jailors to slap her face twenty times.

Cabbage cried, "No. I have something to say." So the mayor bade the jailors to wait.

"When my husband became sick, I asked Esquire Yang to make a diagnosis.

And he wrote the prescription."

"Where is the prescription now?"

"At home." the mayor ordered Cabbage to be put back in the

cell, and he sent one of his men to her home. The shop was closed up and the door had been locked up by the police. The mayor's agent man found a policeman to open the door for him. He went in and searched the place and found the prescription on the table in the bedroom.

At the second interrogation, the mayor said, "Arsenic is not on the prescription. Why did you say Yang poisoned your husband?"

"He wouldn't have written 'arsenic' on the prescription, but he got the medicine for me from the drugstore." She clung to the belief that Esquire Yang would not be executed, even if he were convicted in this sordid tale, because he had an honorary title. Is a title a strong enough amulet to defy death? She had misgivings, but she did not see that she had much choice. Human beings are selfish. To save their own skin, they are usually quite capable of exposing the skin of others. Esquire Yang didn't suspect a thing when the police came to his house. He thought that he would be questioned, or some mistake had been made, and he would soon be back home after giving some explanations. But when Yang was taken into the yamen, the mayor didn't ask him any questions. He just told Yang to write a statement, confessing to what Cabbage had said.

Of course, Yang would not comply. The mayor told the jailors to bring Cabbage in as a witness. He made her repeat what she had said: not one word more, not one word less; and she mumbled out the story.

Yang shouted, "Why are you framing me?" But Cabbage was whisked back to her cell as soon as she finished speaking.

Yang was tortured. He would not admit that he was guilty of the crime. He was tortured more than once; his knee caps were broken. He had to write and sign a statement of confession in the hope that when he appealed to the higher government, this wrong would be righted. He and Cabbage were both sentenced to death, and the mayor sent a report to be approved by the Judicial Ministry, stating that the motive behind the crime was that the husband had found out their adultery.

Yang appealed. The higher government sustained the original verdict: after all, the mayor had bribed them from time to time. Yang then appealed to the governor, who did the same, for the same reason.

Yang had an older sister. The sister had been a wet nurse in the household of a prince. When the bad news reached her, she went to beg her former mistress, the wife of the prince, to spare her brother's life. The wife spoke to the prince about it. The prince told the elder sister to file in an appeal with the Judicial Ministry, and in the meantime he undertook to speak with the minister.

The sister got someone to write up an appeal for her. She hid the written statement in the innermost pocket of her clothes and went to the Judicial Ministry yamen. As part of the appeals process, a bit like a witch's trial, she would have to throw herself on a fateful piece of wood with nails sticking out, to prove that she was honest. She dressed herself in the thickest garments she could find, and set out. When she reached the yamen, she beat the drum at the entrance, indicating that someone had come to sue or to appeal. When the drum-beating was finished, one of the policemen guarding the yamen put out a wooden piece at the gate for her to fling herself on. So she shut her eyes and cast herself on the sharp nails. She held her head high so that her face would not be injured. The sharp ends of the nails penetrated her thick clothes and scratched her skin. Some blood oozed out, but other than that, she was fine. Two policemen helped her to her feet.

Then she took out the appeal from her inner pocket and gave it to a policeman, who took it in to the minister. After a period of time, the minister summoned the sister in. This meant that he had accepted her appeal. The sister knelt before the minister and said, "My brother is a scholar. He could never kill anyone, not even a hen." The minister kept his own counsel, as he was not yet familiar with the details of the case. He dismissed the sister and ordered all the individuals involved in the case to be brought from the town to the capital, to the Judicial Ministry yamen.

The town was in a far southern province. It took more than a month for the concerned parties to travel the long distance to the capital. When the minister questioned Cabbage, she was consistent with what she had said. The son of the mayor had warned her that if she changed anything in her statement, the consequence would be dire. He hadn't explained how dire; but

Cabbage hadn't doubted it. She was totally dependent upon him now and had no idea how to proceed on her own.

The minister had a meeting with his consultants. They all knew that if Cabbage insisted on standing by her confession, they couldn't change the verdict. They had no reason to do so. They had to find a way out. They thought and thought. Finally, one of the councilors said he had an idea.

In a small room of the Judicial Ministry building stood a square table. Two people sat opposite each other. One was Little Cabbage and the other was Yang. They had been brought together in this room by the jailors, who told them that the minister was giving them dinner because they would be executed the next day. They were offered this chance to bid an eternal adieu to each other. There were four dishes on the table, and even wine. Yang was in despair; how unfair this all was. He hadn't murdered anybody. Cabbage hung her head low, ashamed of herself for framing Yang.

At first, both of them were silent. Neither one cared to speak. To break the awkwardness, Yang began, "Well, Cabbage, let's drink farewell, then. We may meet in the next life."

Cabbage could think of nothing to say. So she just hung her head and blushed more. She finally realized that she had been taken in by the mayor's son. It dawned on her that perhaps, he had never loved her at all. But why had he wanted her husband out of the way? She was still naïve and could not believe a man could be such a scoundrel. She had grown up with honorable people like Yang, after all.

"Cabbage," Yang went on, "We will die tomorrow. Can you tell me the truth so that I won't die in ignorance?"

Cabbage thought — what was the use, now, even if she told the truth. They would be executed the next day, all the same. So she made no answer, still hanging her head low.

Yang was a couple of years older than she. They had grown up together in the same neighborhood. They used to play together. Then Yang reached the age to be tutored, and he was generous in transferring his new knowledge to her, teaching her how to read and write. Because her family was not rich, Yang's father would not consent to their marrying; so she was married to the late husband.

"Do you remember when we read the story 'West Chamber' together?" How could she forget? She recalled many scenes from their childhood and adolescence. She almost buried her chin in her chest. "Cabbage, speak to me, please. Let me hear your voice once more before I die." Yang was practically begging her. Her tears dripped on her lap. "Don't cry, Cabbage. Talk to me. We have only tonight to live," Yang said, softly.

Cabbage sobbed out the words, "I'm so sorry."

"No need to say sorry," Yang sighed.

After a while, Cabbage asked bashfully, "Do you hate me?"

"No. Why should I hate you? Everyone will die sooner or later," Yang said philosophically.

"Because I framed you." At last, she had said it.

"So, you did frame me?" Yang said without any surprise. Cabbage nodded.

"Now, tell me the truth, please."

"What's the use, now?"

"At least I should know the truth, before I die."

After further prodding from Yang, Cabbage told him everything. Yang sighed and laughed and began to eat and drink. Presently, a jailor came into their room, holding a stack of paper in his hand. He told Cabbage to sign on the bottom of the last page. Cabbage didn't know what that meant, but she signed anyway. Why should she care what papers she signed? She was about to die. Nothing mattered anymore.

Next day, both of them were brought before the minister. They thought the minister would send them to the execution grounds. But the minister asked Cabbage, "Why didn't you tell the truth in the local government? Or, at least, in the governor's yamen?" Cabbage was confused. She was at a loss to understand what the minister had just asked. She still did not realize the ruse they had used to draw the truth out of her. The minister himself had hidden in the next room with some of his councilors. They had overheard every word murmured between Yang and Cabbage. And a scribe had written down all that Cabbage had confessed to Yang.

The minister issued an order to fetch the mayor, the mayor's son, and the owner of the drugstore who had sold the arsenic to the son. When the drugstore owner pointed to the mayor's son, not to Yang, as the man who had come to him to buy the arsenic, the son could no longer deny his crime. The verdict was overthrown and the son was executed. The mayor was removed from his office and exiled to a remote province. Cabbage and Yang were proved not guilty, and were released. Yang went back to his home in the southern provinces, with permanently crippled knees.

The case was closed. Many officials in that southern province were demoted or dismissed from their posts altogether because they had misjudged a case and jeopardized two innocent lives. The minister wrote a report to West Empress Dowager. She was interested in the case and was curious to see what Cabbage looked like; she summoned Cabbage to her presence. Under ordinary circumstances, only courtiers above a certain rank could be presented to an empress dowager, but Cabbage was a special case. After the interview, Cabbage became a nun.

Printed in the United States
By Bookmasters